CONTENTS

D1437689

PREFACE TO THE FIRST EDITION

The seed for this book was planted whilst preparing my lectures to the nursing students at Waterford Institute of Technology. During my research, it soon became apparent that whilst there were a number of contemporary English and American legal texts written for nurses, the only Irish text was completely out of date, and not in keeping with a four-year degree course.

Whilst it is hoped that this text will go some way toward filling that gap, this work was written with a motive that goes beyond supplying students with an accessible reference when the time comes to research their assignments or swot for their exams.

The message in this book is that nurses are skilled professionals, and it is high time that the related professions, and indeed the country as a whole, recognised this fact. Our nursing students work extremely hard for four years, both in the classroom and in the hospital ward, and emerge with the degree of Bachelor of Science in Nursing. And yet, even with this degree in hand, they are often relegated in their working lives to little more than skivvies to their seemingly more illustrious medical colleagues.

Clearly, in any profession one always starts at the bottom and works upward on the professional ladder. But what constitutes the bottom rung of that ladder should be determined by one's initial qualifications and experience. Our newly qualified nurses enter the professional ranks with an excellent and prestigious degree, and have also completed a substantial number of clinical hours (well in excess of the EU requirement) as part of their studies. They are entitled to the status and privileges enjoyed by other professions with equivalent qualifications and experience, particularly when one considers that many of the everyday duties performed by a nurse are onerous in the extreme.

The United Kingdom is already implementing the process of delegating to nurses some of the tasks previously the preserve of doctors, and it is hoped that Ireland will do the same. Our doctors, particularly junior doctors in State hospitals, often labour under demanding and exhausting workloads. Mistakes are made, and patients ultimately suffer. This makes no sense when in those same hospitals there are a number of nurses who are more than capable of assuming some of those responsibilities.

It is hoped that this book, in some small way, will make people appreciate the enormous reservoir of skill and expertise that is our nursing profession, and I salute the nurses in this country for the fine job that they are performing. May this book be of some use to you.

The law is stated as it was on 31 December 2004.

PREFACE TO THE SECOND EDITION

It is gratifying to see that since the first edition of this book, and the comments therein about nurses being given the recognition that they deserve, things have indeed improved for the nurse in Ireland. Slowly nurses are achieving their deserved position in the health system and gaining the admiration of 'their more illustrious medical colleagues'.

The advent of the registered nurse prescriber is the most tangible of these changes and I hope we will soon see the development and subsequent recognition of another critically important profession, that of the midwife.

This edition has been shortened by economic dictates (and the energy of the author), but I hope that it will again serve the needs of student nurses and those who are already in the profession.

My thanks to the wonderful people at Gill & Macmillan, with whom it is such a pleasure to work. A special mention must be made of Jennifer Armstrong, who showed extraordinary dedication and energy in proofreading my manuscript. Special thanks also to Joanne Cleary-Holdforth for her helpful comments and suggestions. Finally, my thanks to my good friend Gerry Smith, who gets me to work safely every day.

I dedicate this to the person who makes all things possible, my lovely Fiona.

TABLE OF CASES

TABLE OF STATUTES

STATUTORY INSTRUMENTS

EUROPEAN LEGISLATION

THE HIERARCHY AND JURISDICTION OF THE COURTS OF IRELAND

> *Learning outcomes*
> At the completion of this chapter the reader should know and understand:
> * Core legal concepts that are often used in this book.
> * The difference between the criminal courts and the civil courts.
> * The courts system in Ireland and what the different courts can and cannot do.
> * The roles of some of the people who work in the courts system.

Core Concepts

The contents of this book will be easier to understand if you first read this short explanation about how the court system works in Ireland and become familiar with the following terms and concepts.

Hierarchy

Generally, any system of grades or ranks in which some are superior to others. What is meant by the hierarchy of courts is the position of the courts with reference to each other, starting at the bottom all the way to the top. See Figure 1 below.

Precedents

Previous decisions of the superior courts which contain a legal principle that may be referred to and may influence a court's decision in any later case raising the same point of law.

Bind a court

Where a court must follow a previous decision or precedent. Lower courts must follow the decisions of higher courts, whether they agree with the decision or not, as they are 'bound' by the decisions of superior courts.

Adversarial

The Irish legal system is predominantly adversarial, which means it is characterised by its confrontational nature. Parties directly oppose each other and there will be a 'winner' and a 'loser'. A contrasting alternative is the inquisitorial system, where the proceedings are conducted by the presiding officer in the form of an investigation rather than a direct contest.

Pleadings

Formal written or printed statements delivered by litigating parties to each other and which state the allegations of fact and principles of law upon which the parties base their case. They ensure that nobody is caught by surprise on the day of the court hearing, as the parties have been forewarned about their opponent's arguments and have had time to prepare a reply.

Injunction

An order of the court directing a party to do something (mandatory injunction) or to refrain from doing something (prohibitory injunction).

Burden of proof

The burden of proof (onus) needs to be satisfied by the person bringing the claim or laying the charge in order to be successful in that action or charge. A plaintiff in a civil action bears the onus to prove his or her claim on a balance of probabilities, whereas in criminal proceedings the State bears the onus of proving the guilt of the accused beyond a reasonable doubt.

Indictable and summary offences

An indictable offence is one that is sufficiently serious to warrant a jury trial (and heavy sentences), whereas a summary offence (often called a misdemeanour in other jurisdictions) is one that can be heard by a judge alone, with correspondingly lighter sentences.

Acquitted

When the accused (the defendant) is found 'not guilty' in a criminal trial, he or she is said to have been acquitted.

Citation

A reference to an authority (for example, a reported judgment) usually in support of an argument or another judgment. For example, *Walsh v Family Planning Services Ltd* [1992] 1 IR 496 is a citation of a judgment where the plaintiff was Walsh, the defendant was Family Planning Services, and the case can be found on page 496 of the first volume of the 1992 edition of the Irish Reports (IR), as opposed to the Irish Law Reports Monthly (ILRM).

Not all judgments are reported. Generally the citation for an unreported judgment will tell you the date of the decision and the name of the court making that decision.

Bar

In systems that distinguish between barristers and solicitors, the Bar generally refers to the professional collection of barristers, whilst Side-Bar refers to solicitors.

Jurisdiction

Jurisdiction refers to the extent or territory over which legal or other power extends. For example, people are subject to Irish law when they are physically present in the Republic of Ireland and therefore a decision of an Irish court would not affect citizens of the United States, for instance, unless they were physically present in Ireland.

When speaking about civil and criminal jurisdiction we are talking about what civil and criminal courts can and cannot do and where they can and cannot do it.

Civil Courts and Criminal Courts

It is impossible to understand the structure and functioning of courts without understanding the distinction between a criminal case and a civil case, and the functions and powers of both types of court. The critical differences between the two systems are the nature of the dispute and the mechanisms used.

Civil procedure involves private law disputes, for example personal injury claims (tort) or claims for breach of contract, where one of the parties to the dispute initiates the proceedings. Criminal procedure deals with the processing of some activity regarded as a wrong against society or the public in general, and is thus a public law matter. Criminal prosecutions are generally initiated by the Director of Public Prosecutions or An Garda Síochána. It is possible for individuals to initiate private criminal prosecutions, but these are rare.

The purpose of a civil claim is usually to seek compensation (damages) or some specific relief, such as an injunction, for an individual, whereas the aim of criminal proceedings is to punish wrongdoers. If the defendant is found guilty in a criminal court and sentenced to a fine rather than imprisonment, then that fine is paid to the State as criminal law seeks to protect society as a whole rather than an individual victim.

In general, civil proceedings are initiated by pleadings and criminal proceedings are initiated by a summons and indictment (charge sheet). In civil cases we speak of the plaintiff and the defendant, or perhaps the applicant and the respondent, whereas in criminal cases we speak of the prosecution and the defendant (the accused).

It is possible for the same act to lead to both criminal charges and a civil action. For example, if a driver went through a red traffic light and smashed into another car, the driver might be charged in the criminal court with dangerous driving, but might also be sued in the civil court by the owner of the damaged car for compensation. There was only one act, but it resulted in two types of litigation that ended up in different courts with different questions being asked.

In other words, it is not so much the type of wrongful act that distinguishes the civil from the criminal, but the consequences of that wrongful act. If the wrongful act leads to criminal charges, it is governed by criminal law; if it leads to the wrongdoer being sued for damages or having an injunction taken against him or her or being ordered to perform on a contract, it is governed by civil law.

The final distinction to be made between civil and criminal proceedings relates to the burden of proof, which describes the level of evidence needed to secure a judgment or a conviction. In civil cases any particular issue, as well as the overall question of liability, will be determined on a balance of probabilities, which involves comparing the version of events given by the plaintiff with that given by the defendant. In criminal cases all issues and the question of guilt must be proved beyond reasonable doubt. This higher standard of proof needs to convince the reasonable person, not that the accused is guilty, but rather that there is no reasonable chance that the accused is innocent.

Organisation of the Courts

Figure 1: Organisation of the courts

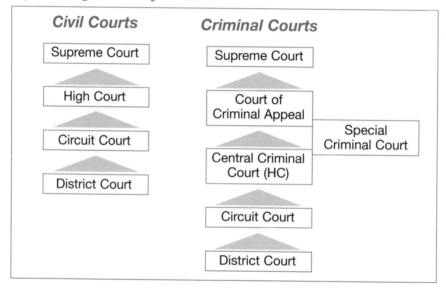

The District Court

The District Court consists of a president and sixty-three ordinary judges. The Republic of Ireland is divided into twenty-four districts, with one or more judges permanently assigned to each district, and the Dublin Metropolitan District. The venue of a District Court case usually depends on where the offence was committed or where the defendant resides, carries on a business or was arrested.

The business of the District Court can be divided into four categories: criminal, civil, family law and licensing. The District Courts are the workhorses of the system. They hear an enormous number of cases, including, for example, actions taken under the Control of Dogs Acts, applications for citizenship, applications to amend birth and marriage certificates and applications under the Environmental Protection Act 1992 (for noise reduction orders).

The District Court is a court of local and limited jurisdiction. This means that it is restricted as to which cases it can decide. As a general rule, a District Court cannot hear a case that has been commenced in a different District Court area or where the damages or compensation sought exceed a certain amount. In criminal matters it is generally restricted to summary offences.

A summary offence, which carries a maximum punishment of twelve months' imprisonment and/or a monetary fine, does not entitle the accused person to a trial by jury. An example would be driving a motor vehicle without insurance. An indictable offence entitles the defendant to a trial by jury, unless the accused agrees to a summary trial where the court is of the opinion that the offence is minor. In such cases the maximum punishment is two years' imprisonment (or twelve months' imprisonment for one offence) and/or a monetary fine. An example here would be assault.

In serious criminal cases, for example murder or rape, the District Court may conduct a preliminary hearing to decide whether there is sufficient evidence to commit the accused for trial by jury before a higher court.

The Circuit Court

The Circuit Court consists of a president and thirty-seven ordinary judges. The President of the District Court is *ex officio* (by virtue of the office) an additional judge of the Circuit Court. The country is divided into eight circuits with one judge assigned to each circuit, except in Dublin where ten judges may be assigned and in Cork where there is provision for three judges. There are twenty-six Circuit Court offices throughout the Republic.

The work of the Circuit Court can be divided into four main areas: civil, criminal, family law and jury service.

The Circuit Court is also a court of local and limited jurisdiction. This means that it is restricted as to which cases it can decide. As a general rule, a Circuit Court in one county cannot hear a case that commenced in another county.

Civil cases in the Circuit Court are tried by a judge sitting without a jury and are restricted to cases where the damages or compensation sought do not exceed a certain amount. There is a right of appeal against the decision of the judge to the High Court, and a Circuit Court judge may consult the Supreme Court on points of law. An unsuccessful party in a District Court civil case can appeal to the Circuit Court, which will re-hear the case and may substitute its own opinion.

In criminal cases the Circuit Court judge sits with a jury of twelve. The criminal jurisdiction is exercised by the judge of the circuit in which the offence was committed or where the defendant (the accused) resides, carries on business or was arrested. However, the judge may transfer a criminal trial from one part of his or her circuit to another. On application by the Director of Public Prosecutions or the accused, the judge may, if satisfied that it would be manifestly unjust not to do so, transfer the trial from a Circuit Court sitting outside the Dublin Circuit to the Dublin Circuit Court.

The High Court

The High Court consists of a president and thirty-six ordinary judges. The President of the Circuit Court and the Chief Justice are *ex officio* additional judges of the High Court.

Normally the High Court sits in Dublin to hear original actions (cases that begin in the High Court rather than appeals from a lower court), but it also sits in the other counties during the year.

The jurisdiction of the High Court extends to all matters, whether of law or fact, civil or criminal. It also has jurisdiction to hear constitutional challenges (usually by citizens) to statutes (with the Supreme Court having appellate jurisdiction in these matters).

The High Court can award unlimited damages.

When the High Court hears a criminal case, it sits as the **Central Criminal Court** and tries only serious offences such as murder or rape. It also tries cases that have been transferred from the Circuit Court to avoid trial before a local jury.

The High Court possesses supervisory jurisdiction over the inferior courts, State bodies and individuals. It has the power to issue an order of:

- Prohibition: to prevent a person or body from exercising a power it does not legally have.
- Mandamus: to compel a person or body to carry out a legal duty.
- Certiorari: to investigate or challenge a person or body who has exceeded their legal powers.
- Habeas corpus: to require the person in custody and the detainer to come before the High Court to explain the circumstances of, and justification for, the detention.

The High Court acts as an appeal court from the Circuit Court in civil matters. It has power to review the decisions of all inferior courts by judicial review and can also review the decisions of certain tribunals of inquiry. It may give rulings on a question of law submitted by the District Court and may hear appeals in certain other circumstances provided by statute (for example, in regard to decisions of the District Court on applications for bail).

The Court of Criminal Appeal

This court hears appeals from the Circuit Court, Central Criminal Court or **Special Criminal Court** (a non-jury court that may be set up under Part V of the Offences Against the State Act 1939). The court consists of three judges, one from the Supreme Court and two from the High Court, with the decision of the court by majority.

The Supreme Court

Article 34 of Bunreacht na hÉireann (the Irish Constitution) states that the courts system in Ireland will include a 'Court of Final Appeal'. This court is the Supreme

Court. It is known as the Supreme Court for the simple reason that it is at the top of the hierarchy of courts. It is the court of final resort for cases that began in the High Court, as well as for those cases that have made their way upwards to the High Court or that were directly appealed on a point of law to the Supreme Court.

The Supreme Court, which is located in Dublin, consists of the Chief Justice and seven ordinary judges. In addition, the President of the High Court is *ex officio* a member of the Supreme Court.

The Supreme Court has the power to hear appeals from all decisions of the High Court and it may hear an appeal from the Court of Criminal Appeal if that court or the Attorney General certifies that the decision involves a legal point of exceptional public interest. The Supreme Court may also give a ruling on a question of law submitted to it by the Circuit Court.

The Constitution provides that the President of Ireland may refer any Bill (or any provision(s) of a Bill) for adjudication to the Supreme Court. The Supreme Court will then decide whether a proposed law is in agreement with, or repugnant to, the Constitution. For this type of case a quorum of five judges will sit, but there will be a single (unanimous) judgment. Once the Supreme Court declares a Bill to be constitutional, the decision is final and the constitutionality of that Bill can never be challenged again. If the Supreme Court declares the Bill to be unconstitutional, then the Oireachtas will have to repair the problems in the Bill that were raised by the court.

If a question of the permanent incapacity of the President of Ireland arises, this is decided by the Supreme Court, again by five judges.

Officers of the Courts

Judges

Article 35.1 of the Constitution says that judges must be appointed by the President of Ireland. In practice, the President appoints judges on the advice of the government, which in turn is guided by the recommendations of the Judicial Appointments Advisory Board.

A qualified barrister or solicitor who has practised as such for not less than ten years is qualified to be appointed as a judge of the District Court or the Circuit Court. A judge of the Circuit Court of four years standing is qualified for appointment as a judge of the High Court or the Supreme Court.

A judge must be free of any political influence, particularly from the government. Article 34.5.1 of the Constitution sets out the sworn oath to be taken by judges, including the well-known phrase 'without fear or favour, affection or ill-will', which underlines the importance of an independent judiciary. Two further practical elements in the independence of the judges of the High Court and the Supreme Court are the extreme difficulty in removing a judge from office (Article 35.4.1) and the guarantee that a judge's salary cannot be reduced (Article 35.5), which ensure that judges do not feel in any way obliged to the government of the day.

As long as a judge's performance in court is *bona fide* (in good faith), he or she cannot be sued for negligence or defamation. This important common law principle ensures that a judge will act without fear or favour and it has been consistently upheld by Irish courts.

Barristers

The barrister's profession is regulated by The Bar Council. A barrister is essentially a courtroom specialist, skilled in the art of advocacy and argument. A barrister is often instructed or briefed by a solicitor to draft pleadings and other complex legal documents. In a big case, a solicitor may gather the evidence, but will brief a barrister to draft the pleadings, give an advice on proofs (i.e. advise on the prospects of success in light of the available evidence) and present the case in court.

Solicitors

The solicitor's profession is regulated by the Law Society of Ireland, which controls entry to the profession, disciplines its members where necessary and protects the public from unqualified persons. A solicitor frequently does legal work not involving litigation or dispute, for example drafting a will or a contract, or conveyancing immovable property. Where there is litigation, a solicitor often does the ground work: research, correspondence, preparation of documentation and collection of evidence, and attends preliminary hearings. Since 1971 a solicitor may appear alone as an advocate in any court in Ireland. However, in practice, solicitors tend to restrict their appearances to the lower courts and employ a barrister to conduct matters in the superior courts and at trials.

Director of Public Prosecutions (DPP)

This office was established by the Prosecution of Offences Act 1974. Although the DPP is a public servant, he or she should be independent of the government in carrying out the functions of the office. The role of the DPP is to prosecute serious crimes in the name of the people, which essentially amounts to deciding whether to charge a person and, if so, with what crime to charge that person. All decisions to prosecute or not are final once made. The reasons for the decision are not published (although this has changed to a very limited extent and further changes have been suggested).

Attorney General (AG)

This office was created in 1924 and has been preserved by Article 30 of the Constitution. The AG is appointed by the President of Ireland on the nomination of the Taoiseach. The appointment is linked to the office of the Taoiseach to the extent that the AG will resign if the Taoiseach resigns. The AG is a legal adviser to the government, and institutes and defends proceedings to which the State is a party.

Useful websites

The Courts Service of Ireland: www.courts.ie

The Supreme Court of Ireland: www.supremecourt.ie

The Bar Council: www.barcouncil.ie

Law Society of Ireland: www.lawsociety.ie

Office of the Attorney General: www.attorneygeneral.ie

Office of the Director of Public Prosecutions: www.dppireland.ie

Part 1

PROFESSIONAL LIABILITY

chapter 1

STATUTORY DEVELOPMENTS

> *Learning outcomes*
> At the completion of this chapter the reader should know and understand:
> * The structure and divisions of the Nurses Act 1985.
> * The key functions to be performed by the Nursing Board in terms of the Nurses Act 1985.
> * The changes to be introduced by the Nurses and Midwives Bill 2010.

Nurses Act 1985 and Nurses and Midwives Bill 2010

The Nurses Act commenced on 30 December 1985. If the Nurses and Midwives Bill 2010 is passed and becomes law, Section 4 of that Bill expressly revokes the 1985 Act. Until that happens, the 1985 Act remains the law. This chapter will briefly summarise the structure and content of the 1985 Act and compare it with the corresponding provisions in the 2010 Bill.

Interpretation

Part 1 of the 1985 Act is entitled 'Preliminary and General' and contains the very important interpretation section. It is important to look at this section because certain words in the statute may be given specialised meanings that differ from their everyday use. Failure to read these specialised words as they were intended to be used in the Act is likely to result in an incorrect interpretation of the Act. This is true of any Act.

The interpretation section of the 1985 Act is surprisingly small and simple given the size and impact of the Act and most of the definitions are straightforward and require very little comment. This means that most words in the 1985 Act must be given their ordinary meaning.

A midwife is included in the definition of 'nurse', as the profession of midwifery is currently a part of the nursing profession rather than a separate profession. However, the 2010 Bill seeks to change this.

The interpretation section of the 2010 Bill is also relatively easy to understand. One of the notable definitions it contains is 'poor professional performance', which means a failure by a nurse or midwife to meet the standards of competence (whether in knowledge and skill or the application of knowledge and skill or both) that can reasonably be expected of a registered nurse or registered midwife, as the case may be, carrying out similar work. This is very similar to the current common law definition of negligence.

In the 2010 Bill there is no longer a definition of nurse, but rather a definition of 'registered nurse' and 'registered midwife', which is a nurse (or midwife) who is already registered in the Register of Nurses or, after the Bill is passed, who is registered in the register created under the new Act. The definition of midwife will no longer be a part of the definition of nurse, but will have a separate definition.

Part 1 in both the 1985 Act and the 2010 Bill also contains details of the commencement and establishment of the statute and of the other statutes that it repeals (replaces).

An Bord Altranais

Part 2 of the 1985 Act deals with the establishment and regulation of An Bord Altranais (the Nursing Board). The Board is the body that regulates the nursing profession in the Republic of Ireland. It is established by Section 6 of the Act, which summarises its main functions as to:

- Promote high standards of education and training in the nursing profession (for example, drawing up syllabi and exit qualifications, and post-registration training).
- Promote high standards of professional conduct among nurses (this would include questions of discipline and punishment related to the operation of the fitness to practise procedures).
- Fulfil the other functions assigned to it by the Act (the most important being the maintenance of the Register of Nurses and the compliance with European Union Directives relating to nursing and midwifery).

Section 6(2) creates what is known in law as a **juristic person**. It is necessary to distinguish between two classes of legal subject. The first is that of human beings or 'natural persons' and the second is juristic persons. All human beings have the capacity to be the possessors of rights and duties and are therefore legal subjects. Juristic persons are devices created by the law that, although they are not human beings, are still recognised by the law as legal subjects with rights and duties but are not treated exactly the same as flesh and blood persons.

For the purposes of business and public necessity, the law recognises a business entity or community or group of persons as having a legal personality, which in turn means that it can have rights and duties. The fact that this device can have rights and duties means that it can participate in administrative, political, economic and other activities, alongside other persons, in its own name. A company is probably the best-known example of a juristic person; a university is another. Both consist of two or more persons or groups of persons – a company of its shareholders and a university of its council, senate, convocation, principal, lecturers and students; but both are legal entities or persons in their own right and legally separate from the people who make them up.

The Act creates the Nursing Board as a juristic person. This means that the Board will continue to exist even though its members may change (after each election) or where a member dies or retires and is replaced. This is because the Nursing Board is regarded as a person in its own right and does not depend for its continued existence on the human beings who serve on the Board. This extended 'life' is known as perpetual succession.

The other important consequence of the Nursing Board being a juristic person is that it can buy and sell land and other property in its own name rather than in the name of the people who serve on the Board. If the land or property was in the names of the people who serve on the Board, it would mean that all the documentation relating to the land and property would need to be altered and new names inserted every time the people serving on the Board changed. There is only one name on the documents that record the ownership of the land and other property and that is of the Nursing Board itself as it is a recognised person capable of owning property.

Finally, because it is recognised as a person in the eyes of the law, the Board can sue, and be sued, in its own name. It is not necessary to sue all the individuals who serve on the Board.

A new Board, Bord Altranais agus Cnáimhseachais na hÉireann, or the Nursing and Midwifery Board of Ireland, will be created to replace the existing Nursing Board under Part 2 of the 2010 Bill. Section 6 of the Bill provides that the previous Board will 'continue in being' but its functions will be taken over by the new Board. In other words, the Bill is seeking a seamless transfer of powers and duties from the old Nursing Board to the new Nursing and Midwifery Board.

Section 8 of the Bill provides:

> The object of the Board shall be the protection of the public in its dealing with nurses and midwives and the integrity of the practice of nursing and midwifery through the promotion of high standards of professional education, training and practice and professional conduct among nurses and midwives.

This theme of protecting the public as regards the activities of nurses and midwives is a strong and recurrent theme in the Bill.

The new Board will perform similar functions to the old Board. Some of the notable functions are the maintenance of the Register of Nurses as well as introducing measures to streamline the registration procedure; the education of nurses and guidance on professional conduct and ethics; overseeing the creation of a new statutory framework dealing with the ongoing professional competence of nurses and midwives and the setting of standards and criteria for specific occupations within the nursing and midwife profession; the establishment of committees to enquire into complaints, with the emphasis on public hearings; the making of decisions and the giving of direction regarding the imposition of sanctions on nurses and midwives; and advising the public.

Section 9(3) of the Bill instructs the Board, within twelve months of the commencement of the new Act, to 'publish in the prescribed manner a code of practice regarding its interactions with nurses and midwives, candidates and members of the public'.

Membership of the Nursing Board

The Nursing Board consists of twenty-nine members. Seventeen of these members (i.e. a clear majority) are nurses elected by nurses. The Minister for Health appoints the other twelve members, one of whom must also be a nurse, which means that at any one time there are at least eighteen nurses on the Board. The ministerial appointees ensure that the government, the medical profession and the public are also represented on the Board.

The seventeen elected nursing representatives are drawn from the demarcated disciplines of general nursing, paediatric nursing, psychiatric nursing, intellectual disability nursing and midwifery. In turn, these disciplines are represented by representatives from the functional sections of training, general administration and clinical practice. Accordingly, the entire nursing profession is properly represented, ensuring that there is not a dominance of interest in favour of one discipline or one function within the profession.

Section 22 of the 2010 Bill creates a smaller Nursing and Midwifery Board of twenty-three persons. Eleven of the members will be either registered nurses or registered midwives; this group shall consist of two academics, one director of nursing/midwifery and eight registered nurses/midwives. Twelve of the members shall not be nurses or midwives; this group shall consist of one doctor, one academic, two persons nominated by the Health Service Executive (HSE), one person nominated by the Council of Health and Social Care Professionals, one person nominated by the Health Information and Quality Authority (HIQA), one person from the voluntary sector and five other persons appointed by the Minister for Health. In other words, the nurses and midwives on the Board will be outnumbered by people who are not nurses or midwives. The Fitness to Practise Committee will also have a majority of people who are not nurses or midwives.

Committees of the Nursing Board

Section 13 of the 1985 Act authorises the Nursing Board to form committees, which can consist of Board members and other people with relevant expertise who are appointed onto these committees. The exception to this rule is the Fitness to Practise Committee (subsection 2), which must comprise only Board members (subsection 5), at least half of whom must be elected Board members (who are themselves nurses) and at least one-third must be appointed Board members. Finally, the chairperson of the committee cannot be the chairperson or vice-chairperson of the Board.

Under the 2010 Bill, the Fitness to Practise Committee (FPC) must have a majority of non-nurses/midwives. Section 24(10) of the Bill stipulates that at least one-third of the members of the FPC, including the chairperson, shall be members of the Board, whilst 'the majority of the membership of that committee shall consist of persons who are not and never have been registered nurses or registered midwives'. The section goes on to say that at least one-third of the membership of the FPC shall consist of registered nurses or registered midwives.

This could mean that the entire committee could be Board members as long as there is a majority of non-nurses and non-midwives. One would hope, however, that there will be some outside appointments of persons without any connection to the Board. The wording used in the Bill should allow this, thereby avoiding the current situation where the committee is composed entirely of Board members.

The 2010 Bill also provides for the creation of two new committees. The first is the Preliminary Proceedings Committee (PPC), which is to give initial consideration to complaints made against registered nurses and midwives. This is in essence a screening mechanism to decide whether complaints should be pursued further. The workings of this committee, detailed in Part 7 of the Bill, are intended to ensure that proceedings leading up to a charge of being unfit to practise will be carried out in accordance with the rules of natural justice. The PPC must also ensure that complaints are dealt with expeditiously and that the complainant is kept up to date with developments. These measures are presumably a response to the criticism levelled at the Board by the superior courts hearing the applications brought by Ann O'Ceallaigh against the Board and the FPC (see Chapter 2).

The other new committee is the Midwives Committee, which is to advise the Board on all matters pertaining to midwifery. It will consist of at least five members: one must be a registered midwife who is a member of the Board; at least four other persons must be appointed by the Board, and these four persons must consist of two midwives, including one who is a self-employed community midwife; a registered medical practitioner who is a specialist gynaecologist; and a representative of the public who is not a nurse or a midwife.

The Bill seeks to recognise and regulate midwifery as a separate and distinct profession from nursing. This is what it says in the long title. However, there are very few details in the Bill as to how this objective is to be achieved. Section 2(2) of the Bill states: 'For the avoidance of doubt, it is hereby declared and recognised that midwifery is a separate profession to nursing.' Apart from that statement, there is nothing else said about how this separation is going to take place.

There have always been separate divisions in the Register of Nurses, and the new Board is to consist of both nurses and midwives and is to deal with both professions, so what has actually changed? It may well be that the Midwives Committee will be the committee to watch, as it is likely to be the driving force behind the move to separate nursing and midwifery as distinct and independent professions. It is to be hoped that it will formulate policies and practices to ensure this.

The 2010 Bill says that the Board may, but does not have to, establish an Education and Training Committee to oversee the education and training of nurses, midwives and candidates. It may also establish a Health Committee to provide support and assistance to nurses and midwives with disabilities.

Fees charged by the Nursing Board
The Nursing Board generates its own income by charging nurses to register, to continue being registered and to re-register where necessary. The Board also

charges fees for the certificate of registration, registration as a trainee nurse, examinations and training.

Section 38 of the 2010 Bill continues this tradition and authorises the Board to charge fees for essentially the same sort of things as are provided for in the 1985 Act.

Nurses Rules

The Nursing Board is empowered by the 1985 Act to make rules for the purposes of the operation of the Act, for example regarding committees and their membership and functions. The 'Nurses Rules, 2010' begins:

> An Bord Altranais in exercise of the powers conferred on it by Sections 11, 26, 27, 28, 31, 32 and 33 of the Nurses Act, 1985, and by Statutory Instrument, S.I. No. 3 of 2010, Health (An Bord Altranais)(Additional Functions) Order 2010 hereby makes the following Rules.

Section 13 of the 2010 Bill similarly authorises the Board to make rules. This is an extensive section and the new Board will be authorised to make rules regulating, among other things: the running of its committees; the creation and maintenance of the register of nurses and midwives; the candidate register and the advanced nurse practitioner (ANP)/advanced midwife practitioner (AMP) posts register and its divisions; the payment of fees; the receiving and recording by the PPC or the FPC of evidence and/or submissions; the creation and administration of subcommittees of the committees; the setting of criteria for the purposes of education and training; the setting of criteria or conditions for persons who wish to practise nursing or midwifery after having not practised for a period specified in the rules; clinical supervising authorities for midwives; any professional competence scheme; and any other matter relating to the Board's functions.

Generally, the Board must have the approval of the Minister for Health before it can make any rules. The draft form of these rules should be published for comment by interested parties before being finalised and implemented. The Minister will cause any proposed rule to be placed before the Oireachtas, which may annul it if it does not agree with the proposal.

Section 14 of the 2010 Bill authorises the Board to prepare guidelines, consistent with the Act, for the guidance of nurses and midwives and the public.

Registration

One of the Nursing Board's most important functions is the registration of newly qualified nurses and the re-registration of existing nurses. There is also the question of recognising nurses who have trained and qualified in countries other than Ireland. Part 3 of the 1985 Act deals with the question of registration and the maintenance of the Register of Nurses. The register is divided up into appropriate sections or divisions, determined by specialisation, including a division for midwives.

Section 27 of the 1985 Act instructs the Board to prepare, establish and maintain the register, and thereafter to publish it 'at such times and in such manner as the Minister may direct'. A nurse must notify the Board if there are any changes in his or her name or address. The Board must furnish a nurse with a certificate once his or her registration is complete; the certificate is evidence (including evidence in legal proceedings) that the person named is a registered nurse, until the contrary is shown. The clear intention behind Section 27 is that the Board must maintain a 'live' register, in other words a register that is accurate and up to date, with the names and addresses of all current nurses. The names of persons who have retired, died, failed to pay their retention fee or been declared unfit should be removed.

Section 28 of the Act instructs the Board to register every person who complies with the prescribed conditions for registration, in other words everyone who is a qualified nurse or midwife, including nurses and midwives from other European Union (EU) countries. A nurse with two or more qualifications can be registered in more than one division of the register.

Section 29 instructs the Board to correct the register from time to time, which means that the Board must maintain the register, ensuring its accuracy. Any person who is affected by a correction must be notified and given a chance to correct any further errors.

Section 30 deals with the registration of persons in ancillary professions. This section is essentially defunct as there is now specialist legislation dealing with the registration of professions traditionally seen as ancillary to the nurse's profession, for example social carers and social workers.

According to the 'Nurses Rules, 2010', the register is made up of the following divisions:

- General Nurses Division (RGN).
- Psychiatric Nurses Division (RPN).
- Children's Nurses Division (formerly the Sick Children's Nurse Division) (RCN).
- Intellectual Disability Nurses Division (formerly the Mental Handicap Nurse Division) (RNID).
- Midwives Division (RM).
- Public Health Nurses Division (RPHN).
- Nurse Tutors Division (RNT).
- Nurse Prescribers Division (RNP).
- Advanced Nurse Practitioner Division (RANP).
- Advanced Midwife Practitioner Division (RAMP).

The 2010 Bill continues to recognise the importance of the registration functions carried out by the Board and Part 6 of the Bill is entirely devoted to the registration of nurses and midwives. This extensive part of the new Bill deals with the creation and maintenance of the current register, and the creation and maintenance of divisions within that register, including the advanced nurse practitioner division and the advanced midwife practitioner division.

Section 50 of the Bill provides for the candidate register, and the wording of that section seems to indicate that this register is separate from the nurses and midwives register, rather than being a division of that register.

Education and training

Part 4 of the 1985 Act deals with one of the most important functions carried out by the Board, namely the education and training of nurses. Sections 31 and 32 allow the Board to make rules for training courses and examinations for candidate nurses and for existing nurses, including rules governing approval of lecturers and teachers, admission to examinations and the granting of certificates to successful candidates. As a rule, the Board does not train and examine directly, but rather appoints other institutions for this purpose.

Section 33 of the Act allows the Board to hold examinations. Again, these are not held by the Board directly, but usually by appointed institutions. These approved institutions are appointed by the Board in terms of Section 34. Section 35 allows the Board to stipulate the minimum educational requirements necessary for entry for training as a nurse. Section 36 instructs the Board to review, at least once every five years, the standards (of both exams and clinical training), the curricula and the suitability of institutions to train candidate nurses. Section 37 instructs the Board to ensure that the training of Irish nurses will satisfy the minimum standards specified in any EU Directive or Regulation.

Part 10 of the 2010 Bill deals with the education and training of midwives. Section 86 sets out the duties of the HSE, as opposed to the Nursing Board, in that regard. Section 86 begins with the following paragraph: 'The Health Service Executive, in accordance with section 7(4)(b) of the Health Act 2004, shall, as far as practicable, facilitate the education and training of candidates.' The remainder of the section details the duties of the HSE 'with respect to specialist nursing and midwifery education and training'. Accordingly, the HSE now has duties to educate and train a specific sector of nurses and midwives, namely specialists in those fields.

Section 87 of the Bill sets out the duties of the Board in regard to the education and training of nurses and midwives. These duties are very similar to those set out in the 1985 Act.

Discipline and sanctions

Part 5 of the 1985 Act deals with the question of fitness to practise and the fitness to practise inquiry, which will be examined in Chapter 2.

The 2010 Bill seeks to create improved procedures to investigate complaints against nurses and midwives. The most significant change in this regard is the formation of the Preliminary Proceedings Committee, the workings of which are governed by Part 7 of the Bill and will be dealt with in the next chapter.

Miscellaneous

Part 6 of the 1985 Act is entitled 'Miscellaneous' and is dedicated to tidying up aspects of the Act that needed attention; it is a sort of 'housekeeping' part at the end. Included in Part 6 are details of what happens to people who pretend to be nurses, which is a serious offence.

Part 13 of the 2010 Bill is the Miscellaneous part and includes sections on the duties of clinical supervising authorities, privilege, investigation, prosecution of offences, the power to specify the form of documents and the amendment of the Freedom of Information Act 1997.

Unlike the 1985 Act, the Bill's offences section is no longer in the Miscellaneous part. Section 39 of Part 6 of the Bill (Registration and Practice) deals with the question of unregistered nurses and midwives being forbidden to practise, whilst Section 40 prohibits any person from attending a woman in childbirth for reward unless he or she is a registered midwife or doctor, or a person training to be either a midwife or doctor and who attends the birth as part of that training. The penalties for being convicted under these sections are harsh. If summarily convicted, the person can receive a fine of up to €5,000 or a prison sentence of up to six months, or both. If convicted on indictment, for a first offence the person faces a fine of up to €65,000 and/or prison for up to five years; and for subsequent offences the convicted person faces a fine of up to €160,000 and/or prison for up to ten years.

Section 44 of the 2010 Bill deals with the offence of impersonating a nurse or midwife or falsely representing to be a nurse or midwife. A person convicted of such an offence is liable for the same harsh punishments as those outlined above with regard to Section 40.

Enactment

The government has said that it intends to have the Bill passed as soon as possible. The Bill completed the Second Stage on 27 May 2010 and was referred to Select Committee on the same day. As of September 2010 there have been no further developments.

Statutory developments: summary

1   The Nurses Act 1985 is made up of six parts:
    (a) Part 1 deals with the commencement of the Act, which was on 30 December 1985.
    (b) Part 2 established An Bord Altranais (the Nursing Board) and dissolved the previous Board.
    (c) Part 3 deals with the registration of nurses and the maintenance of the Register of Nurses.
    (d) Part 4 details how the Board is to control the education, training and examination of nurses, primarily through the appointment of institutions that are qualified to carry out these functions.
    (e) Part 5 deals with the question of whether a nurse is fit to practise and the mechanisms provided to determine that question.
    (f) Part 6 deals with miscellaneous matters, including offences.

2   The Nursing Board, created by the Nurses Act 1985, is a juristic person, with rights and duties, and is capable of owning land and property. It continues to exist in its own name when the human beings who make up the Board die or are replaced in elections. It can also sue or be sued in its own name.

3   The most important functions of the Nursing Board are: registration of nurses and the maintenance of the Register of Nurses; controlling the education and training of nurses; the discipline and, if necessary, punishment of nurses; and ensuring that Ireland complies with its obligations as an EU Member State as regards the recognition of qualifications of nurses who have trained outside Ireland but in the EU.

4   The Nurses and Midwives Bill 2010, if passed, will replace the Nurses Act 1985 in its entirety and will create a new board named Bord Altranais agus Cnáimhseachais na hÉireann, or the Nursing and Midwifery Board of Ireland, which has powers to deal with largely the same areas as those detailed above, but with a greater emphasis on mechanisms to ensure accountability of the nursing and midwifery professions to the Irish public.

Further reading

Nurses and Midwives Bill 2010 and the Explanatory Memorandum, both available from the Department of Health's website.

'Nurses and Midwives Bill 2010', *An Bord Altranais News* (summer 2010), 1–2.

O'Dwyer, P. 'Looking back . . . moving forward: the educational preparation of nurses in Ireland', *Nursing Education Perspectives* 28/3 (2007), 136–9.

Troy, P. H., Wyness, L. A. and McAuliffe, E. 'Nurses' experiences of recruitment and migration from developing countries: a phenomenological approach', *Human Resources for Health* 5 (2007), 15.

Useful websites

An Bord Altranais: www.nursingboard.ie
British and Irish Legal Information Institute: www.bailii.org
Department of Health and Children: www.dohc.ie
Government of Ireland: www.gov.ie
Irish Medical Directory: www.imd.ie
Irish Statute Book: www.irishstatutebook.ie

chapter 2

THE FITNESS TO PRACTISE INQUIRY

Learning outcomes
At the completion of this chapter the reader should know and understand:
* The principles of natural justice and the concept of *ultra vires.*
* The procedure to be followed by the fitness to practise inquiry in terms of Section 38 of the Nurses Act 1985.
* The options available to the Nursing Board in terms of Section 44 of the Nurses Act 1985.
* The sanctions that may be imposed on a nurse who is found guilty of misconduct by the inquiry.
* The role of the High Court.
* The changes to be introduced by the Nurses and Midwives Bill 2010.

Introduction

Part 5 of the Nurses Act 1985 is entitled 'Fitness to Practise' and details the disciplinary powers of the Nursing Board and, more specifically, the workings of the Fitness to Practise Committee (FPC).

A nurse can be removed from the Register of Nurses for misconduct or incapacity. It is impossible to define misconduct precisely in the nursing sense, but a starting point may be found in the 'Nurses Rules, 2010' and other professional or ethical guidelines.

Ultra Vires and the Principles of Natural Justice

An internal disciplinary body is governed by administrative law. The most important concepts that need to be remembered when looking at administrative law are the principles of natural justice. Another concept that is important to know about is *ultra vires.*

The principles of natural justice are rules entrenched in the common law. The first important principle of natural justice is *audi alteram partem* (hear the other side), which, in the context of disciplinary hearings, means that anyone whose rights, privileges and liberties are affected by the action of an administrative authority must be given a chance to be heard on the matter. In practice, this means that everyone is entitled to speak in their own defence. When a complaint made against a nurse is placed before the FPC, the nurse has the right to bring forward evidence and witnesses in his or her defence and to inspect and question the evidence and witnesses brought against him or her.

The second important principle of natural justice that is applicable to disciplinary hearings is *nemo judex in sua causa* (no one may be a judge in his own cause). This means that the person or people who sit on the FPC must be independent of both sides and have no interest in the outcome of the hearing. In other words, the committee members must be completely fair and impartial to the nurse who has been accused of misconduct and any members who are unable to be impartial (they may know the nurse well or may have had a previous unpleasant experience with that nurse) must excuse themselves and take no part in the hearing.

Finally, a body created by a statute is only allowed to exercise powers that have been given to it by that statute. As the FPC is created by statute (Nurses Act 1985) it is not allowed to exercise powers that it has not been given by that Act. If it does something that is not provided for by the empowering statute, it will have acted *ultra vires* (outside the law). The nurse on the receiving end of that unlawful exercise of powers could challenge the decision of the FPC before the High Court, through a process known as judicial review. If the nurse is successful, the High Court can reverse the committee's decision.

With these principles in mind, it is necessary to examine the applicable provisions of Part 4 of the Nurses Act 1985.

Procedure in a Fitness to Practise Inquiry

Section 38 of the Nurses Act 1985 is a vitally important section as it lays down the entire procedure to be followed when a complaint is made concerning a nurse's conduct or capacity and raising questions about that nurse's fitness to practise. A complaint against a nurse can be made by 'any person': most often this will be a member of the public (including visitors and relatives of patients), but it could also be a fellow nurse, any other health professional, a patient or perhaps even a lawyer acting on behalf of an unhappy patient.

In addition to complaints of misconduct, Section 38 applies to allegations that a nurse is incapacitated from fulfilling his or her functions and duties by reason of a physical or mental disability. The Nurses and Midwives Bill 2010 says that the Board may create a committee, known as the Health Committee, to support and assist nurses and midwives with disabilities. It will be interesting to see whether this committee is used as an alternative mechanism to the fitness to practise procedure when a nurse or midwife is incapacitated through disability as opposed to misconduct. At the very least it should be a precursor to the FPC, in an attempt to resolve the matter without resorting to adversarial proceedings.

What happens once a complaint is received is essentially a two-step procedure. The FPC must first consider the merits of the complaint and whether the nurse in question has a case to answer – what is known as a *prima facie* case (a case on the face of it). If the FPC feels that there is no substance to a complaint, or that the action of the nurse was so minor that any disciplinary action would be excessive, the matter should end there and then. However, the FPC does not take this decision alone. Instead it must report to the Nursing Board with its recommendation. After considering the recommendation, the Board can either agree that the matter be closed, or disagree and insist that an inquiry be held. It is highly unlikely that the Board would ever refuse to follow the FPC's recommendation, particularly as the FPC consists of Board members.

Section 38 does not instruct the FPC or the Board to notify the nurse about the complaint or to invite the nurse to make representations. It describes this first stage of the process as an internal matter dealt with by the FPC. The nurse who is the subject of the complaint has very little to do with the process at this stage and often is not notified of the complaint until the FPC has decided whether to pursue or discard the complaint.

The Supreme Court criticised this approach in its decision in *O'Ceallaigh v An Bord Altranais* (Unreported, SC, 17 May 2000). It found that there was no express provision in Section 38 for either the Board or the FPC to notify the nurse who is the subject of the complaint before making a decision on whether to establish an inquiry in terms of Section 38. However, despite the wording of Section 38(2), the Supreme Court held that there was a duty to notify the nurse at that stage so that the nurse could respond to the complaint before the decision was taken on whether to establish an inquiry. This is in keeping with the *audi alteram partem* principle, as the decision made by the FPC at that first stage clearly impacts on the nurse concerned and therefore that nurse should be able to have input on the matter under consideration.

In other words, even though Section 38 does not tell the Board to notify the nurse about the complaint and invite representations from the nurse in response to the complaint it does not mean that there is no duty on the Board to do just that. The principles of natural justice are older and more established than the Nursing Act and the Board should not forget these fundamental principles when it interprets the Act. The Supreme Court said that neither the FPC nor the Board could be said to be exercising its power lawfully and fairly without the nurse being informed of the complaint and the FPC and/or the Board having sight of any response to the complaint that the nurse might make before the FPC and/or the Board decided whether to proceed with the inquiry.

This decision is important as it means that a nurse would have an opportunity to stop the matter going any further if he or she could produce evidence at the preliminary stage to show that the complaint had absolutely no merit, rather than having to go through the entire procedure of the inquiry, including the wait before the inquiry. This approach would also force the FPC and the Board to proceed quickly with the formalities if they want to take any action against a nurse. When one considers that Ann O'Ceallaigh, a domiciliary midwife who specialised in homebirths, was suspended for over two years as a result of a complaint, it is easy to see how prejudicial that first stage decision could be to a nurse. It is only proper that the nurse should be able to respond to the complaint as soon as possible.

The Nurses and Midwives Bill 2010 has taken this criticism into account by creating the Preliminary Proceedings Committee (PPC) in Part 7 of the Bill. Section 57 says that the initial complaint against the nurse or midwife will be made to the PPC. Under Section 58, the Board can appoint people to assist the

PPC and these people can interview witnesses, take statements, receive documentary evidence and advise the PPC. Section 59 says that the PPC shall 'consider whether there is sufficient cause to warrant further action being taken in relation to the complaint'.

Importantly, under Section 59(6) to (9) of the Bill, the PPC must notify the nurse or midwife who is the subject of the complaint and supply to that nurse details of the nature of the complaint and the name of the complainant. In response to this, the nurse or midwife may supply to the PPC 'any information that the nurse or midwife believes should be considered by the Committee or the Fitness to Practise Committee'. The PPC may even require the nurse or midwife to supply this information. This will probably become the standard procedure (i.e. the PPC will inform the nurse or midwife about the complaint and the complainant and instruct the nurse or midwife to respond by placing any information before the PPC that he or she wants it to consider). If the nurse or midwife fails or refuses to supply this information, the PPC has at least complied with the principles of natural justice as emphasised by the Supreme Court.

The second step of the procedure under Section 38 of the 1985 Act commences once the FPC and the Board (or the Board alone) decide to proceed with the complaint and hold an inquiry. This operates along the lines of a disciplinary inquiry with the evidence being presented against the nurse or midwife who is the subject of the complaint, and the nurse or midwife being allowed to challenge that evidence and lead evidence of his or her own. The FPC is given the powers possessed by a High Court judge as far as getting witnesses to testify or produce documents. Obviously, the witnesses themselves have the same immunities and privileges as witnesses before the High Court (i.e. they can claim testimonial privilege or privilege against self-incrimination).

In another application brought by Ann O'Ceallaigh – *O'Ceallaigh v Fitness to Practise Committee of An Bord Altranais* (Unreported, SC, 11 December 1998), the Supreme Court held that the nurse or midwife against whom the complaint is brought is entitled to produce expert witnesses to testify in his or her defence and that these witnesses are entitled to be present at the inquiry held in terms of Section 38 of the 1985 Act.

In terms of the 2010 Bill, the FPC comes into the picture only once the PPC and/or the Board has decided that there is a *prima facie* case for the nurse or midwife to answer and refers it to the FPC under Section 63 of the Bill.

Part 8 of the 2010 Bill deals with the conduct and proceedings of the FPC. Section 64 says that once the complaint is referred to the FPC, the chief executive officer of the Board must notify, in writing, the nurse or midwife who is the subject of the complaint. The notice must set out the nature of the complaint, including the particulars of any evidence in support of the complaint; and inform the nurse or midwife of the right to be present, to be represented and to offer a defence against the complaint. The nurse or midwife may request that all or part of the hearing be held in private rather than in public and must give the reasons for that request (what is known as showing reasonable and sufficient cause). It is interesting to note that the witnesses, including the complainant, can also request that some or all of the hearing be heard in private and again they must show reasonable and sufficient cause. The notice must also contain details of the date, time and place of the hearing in sufficient time for the nurse or midwife to prepare for the hearing.

Section 65 of the Bill details how the hearing is to be run. The hearing must be a public hearing unless the FPC decides that there is sufficient cause to hold some or all of the hearing in private. The chief executive officer must present the evidence supporting the complaint, witnesses will testify under oath (or presumably affirmation, which is a secular oath), and there is a right to cross-examine these witnesses and call evidence in reply. As in the 1985 Act, Section 66 of the Bill says that the FPC has all the powers, rights and privileges that are possessed by a High Court judge, including the right to subpoena witnesses, to examine witnesses (and hear evidence orally or by affidavit, CCTV, video recording, sound recording or other format) and to order the production of documents. Similarly, witnesses are entitled to claim the usual privileges and immunities.

Ann O'Ceallaigh raised another important issue concerning the FPC and involving the second principle of natural justice, namely that of *nemo judex in sua causa* (no one may be a judge in his own cause), which in practice means that the person in charge of the inquiry must be seen to be completely neutral and independent without any interest in the outcome of the proceedings. In an application to the High Court – *O'Ceallaigh v An Bord Altranais and Others* (Unreported, HC, 23 October 2009), O'Ceallaigh asked the court to set aside a decision of the FPC on the grounds that the chairperson of the committee hearing the complaint against her could not be objective because one of the witnesses who was giving evidence against her worked in the same hospital (Rotunda) as the chairperson. O'Ceallaigh argued that this created an apprehension of bias as a result of the professional relationship between the chairperson and the witness.

The High Court found that there was no apprehension of bias. The court said that a reasonable person, on the facts before it, would not worry that O'Ceallaigh would not receive a fair and impartial hearing because of the risk of bias on the part of the chairperson. The relationship between the chairperson and the witness was not enough in itself to prove bias. It had to be shown that the circumstances of that relationship and its connection with the proceedings were such that it had the capacity to influence the mind of the decision maker. The relationship must be such that there is 'a community of interest' between them that is directly related to the subject matter of the proceedings for objective bias to arise. This link must be cogent and rational. The fact that the relationship was between the chairperson and a witness, rather than one of the parties before the hearing, meant that the test to establish bias was higher.

This test set out by the High Court to establish an apprehension of bias is extremely strict as it seems to require that the applicant must establish bias rather than an apprehension of bias. We all know the maxim that justice must not only be done, it must be seen to be done. If a reasonable person heard about the relationship between the witness and the chairperson would they think 'that doesn't sound right'? It could be argued that on the facts there is a reasonable apprehension of bias. For example, if the relationship meant that the chairperson automatically believed everything that the witness said, without objectively analysing the testimony of the witness, is that not enough for the chairperson to recuse himself or herself? The question is not whether the chairperson would automatically believe everything that the witness would say, but whether a reasonable person might foresee that there is a danger that that will happen. There is no indication in the judgment as to whether O'Ceallaigh has appealed the decision of the High Court, but perhaps she should.

Sanctions
Erasure or suspension from the register
If the Nursing Board finds that a person is unfit to practise, either because of misconduct or incapacity, it can do one of two things under Section 39 of the 1985 Act. The Board can either remove the nurse from the Register of Nurses altogether (this is called 'erasure' in the section) or suspend the nurse from practising as a nurse for a certain period. The Board has other options when it comes to sanctioning nurses, but these are provided in later sections.

The Board must inform the nurse of its decision in writing and deliver this to the nurse. The nurse has twenty-one days from the date of the decision to challenge it before the High Court, as a matter of judicial review. It is important to note that this time limit starts to run from the date of the decision and not from the date that the news of the decision was received by the nurse.

A nurse proceeds with an application for an appeal by using a special summons and an affidavit (sworn evidence in a document) setting out the nurse's reasons for challenging the Board's decision. The Board will reply to these written representations in its own affidavit. Where there are extraordinary circumstances, for example where a witness was not available at the hearing or there is a dispute about whether a witness told the truth, the High Court can order a full re-hearing of the matter. At this re-hearing the witnesses will again give their evidence, but this time it will be in court. This is what happened in *K v An Bord Altranais* [1990] IR 396.

If a nurse does not apply to the High Court and does not give any indication that he or she intends to challenge the decision of the Board, the Board is entitled to apply to the High Court to confirm its decision. In making such an application, the Board must show that the nurse had an opportunity to be heard, that the finding of the Board was correct and equitable and that the Board is seeking to enforce what is an appropriate punishment.

On reviewing the decision of the FPC and/or the Board, the High Court can do one of three things: agree with the decision and confirm it, disagree with the decision and cancel it or change the decision for one it decides is more appropriate.

The nurse may be given leave to appeal the decision of the High Court to the Supreme Court, but only on a point of law. In other words, if the nurse was arguing that the High Court's interpretation of the Act or the common law was wrong, this could be the basis of an appeal. The nurse cannot appeal the decision just because he or she does not agree with that decision.

Retention on register with conditions

If the Board decides that a removal or suspension from the Register of Nurses is not appropriate on the facts of a proven complaint, Section 40 of the 1985 Act authorises the Board to allow the nurse to continue to practise but with conditions or restrictions on the nurse's freedom to practise. For example, a nurse might be prohibited from doing certain tasks or practising outside a certain area.

If the nurse is unhappy with this decision, the same procedures apply as those described above in relation to Section 39, namely to bring the matter before the High Court on review.

Other sanctions

If the Board decides that removal, suspension or restriction would not be appropriate on the proved facts of the complaint, Section 41 of the 1985 Act allows it to advise, admonish or censure a nurse, which essentially amounts to an official (and therefore recorded) scolding. Interestingly enough, the section does not provide that the nurse can challenge the censure in the High Court. However, if the nurse can show that the censure will have a serious and damaging impact on his or her career, it must be argued that the failure of the legislature to provide for a remedy in the High Court cannot be said to disqualify the nurse from challenging the censure in the High Court.

Section 42 of the 1985 Act says that a nurse can be removed from the register if convicted in the Republic of Ireland of an indictable offence (a criminal offence that is serious enough to warrant a jury trial). If the nurse is convicted in another country of an offence that would be an indictable offence in the Republic of Ireland, then that shall have the same effect and the nurse can be removed from the register. The nurse can challenge such decisions in the High Court, and the same procedures apply as in Sections 39 and 40.

Part 9 of the Nurses and Midwives Bill 2010 details the sanctions that are available to the Board if a complaint is upheld against a nurse or midwife by the FPC and confirmed by the Board. Section 71 says that the Board can decide that one or more of the following sanctions be imposed on the nurse or midwife:

(a) an advice or admonishment, or a censure, in writing;
(b) a censure in writing and a fine not exceeding €2,000;
(c) the attachment of conditions to the nurse's or midwife's registration, including restrictions on the practice of nursing or midwifery that may be engaged in by the nurse or midwife;

(d) the transfer of the nurse's or midwife's registration to another division;

(e) the suspension of the nurse's or midwife's registration for a specified period;

(f) the cancellation of the nurse's or midwife's registration from the register of nurses and midwives or a division of that register;

(g) a prohibition from applying for a specified period for the restoration of the nurse's or midwife's registration in the register of nurses and midwives or a division.

Under Section 73 of the Bill, the Board must notify the nurse or midwife in writing of its decision regarding the sanction, the date on which the decision was made and the reasons for arriving at that decision.

Section 74 says that a decision under Section 71 to impose a sanction (unless it was an advice, admonishment or censure) shall not take effect unless the decision is confirmed by the High Court on an appeal under Section 75 or an application by the Board to confirm under Section 76. This is an important provision as it means that there will always be court involvement when a decision to punish is made by the FPC and the Board acts on that recommendation.

Under Section 75, the nurse or midwife who has been notified of that sanction can appeal to the High Court against the sanction within twenty-one days of receiving the notification. This is the judicial review procedure discussed earlier. Again, the court can confirm, quash or substitute. Section 76 says that even if the nurse or midwife does not appeal the sanction, the Board may apply to the court for confirmation of the decision. This application can be made *ex parte*; in other words, the Board does not have to tell the nurse or midwife concerned that it is going to court to ask for a confirmation in terms of this section. Section 77 authorises the court to hear expert witnesses in a hearing under Sections 75 or 76.

Again, the nurse or midwife can appeal against the decision of the High Court to the Supreme Court, but only on a question of law.

Section 79 authorises the Board to remove a nurse or midwife from the Register of Nurses and Midwives for failing to pay the registration renewal fee, unless that nurse or midwife is the subject of a hearing pursuant to a complaint against him or her. Section 80 says that this removal can be reversed if application is made, and the outstanding fee paid, not later than six months after the fee was due.

If the Board refuses to renew a registration, or attaches conditions to the registration, it must notify the nurse or midwife concerned of the reasons for that refusal or conditions, so as to allow that nurse or midwife to appeal the decision in court within twenty-one days of receiving the notice. Again, the procedure is that of judicial review and the court can confirm, quash or substitute the decision of the Board.

Removal from register for non-payment of fees

Section 47 of the 1985 Act authorises the Board to reinstate a nurse on the Register of Nurses where that nurse's name was deleted from the register as a result of non-payment of fees. The section is clear that this is the only reason the Board can use to reinstate a nurse on the register. In other words, this section does not cover the situation where a nurse was removed for misconduct or incapacity, it applies only where the nurse was removed for not paying the annual fee.

This matter is dealt with by Sections 79 to 81 of the 2010 Bill, which say that nurses or midwives who fail to pay a fee, despite a notice calling on them to do so, may be removed from the register. Restoration of such a registration will be performed by the Board's chief executive officer if the fee is paid within six months of its due date and is accompanied by an application for restoration. Section 83 allows a nurse or midwife to appeal to the High Court against any decision by the Board to remove his or her name from the register for failing to pay a fee.

Immediate Suspension Pending the Fitness to Practise Inquiry

Section 44 of the 1985 Act authorises the Nursing Board to apply to the High Court, before or even during the inquiry, to remove a nurse's name from the Register of Nurses. This is clearly a serious step as it prevents the nurse from practising and therefore earning a living as a nurse. The Board must show the High Court that it would be in the interests of the public to have the nurse's name removed from the register in order to stop that nurse practising.

The Board can approach the High Court on an urgent *ex parte* application, which is an application in the absence of the nurse against whom the complaint was made. This means that the Board can approach the High Court without giving any notice to the nurse that it intends applying to the High Court for his or her removal from the register. This application can be heard *in camera*, which means that no members of the general public are allowed to be present when the application is argued before the judge. The High Court has a very wide discretion in deciding what would be the appropriate thing to do on the facts presented to it.

These are called injunction proceedings as they stop the nurse from practising. They are granted in urgent and serious circumstances where a disciplinary hearing could not act soon enough to prevent harm to the public. In other words, as a person is always presumed innocent until proven guilty, there would need to be clear evidence that the nurse presents a danger to the public and must be stopped immediately.

An injunction hearing is usually a two-stage procedure. As the court might hear only the applicant's version before it grants the injunction, this first injunction is called an interim injunction and is really seen as a temporary or stop-gap measure until the court can hear full arguments from both sides on the 'return day' (the date of the continuation of the hearing). If the court does not stipulate a return day, either the Board or the nurse can apply for one, which should ensure that the matter will be resolved quickly.

Ann O'Ceallaigh, the midwife referred to earlier, was also injuncted (prevented by an injunction) from practising as a midwife, as the Board made a successful application to the High Court for an injunction against her even before the Section 38 hearing started. This so-called interim injunction prevented O'Ceallaigh from practising for two years. When the Board approached the High Court two years later and asked the court to make the injunction a permanent injunction, this application was refused. The court said that the Board should have familiarised itself with the current facts of the case before making the application for a permanent order because a lot of things had changed over the two-year period.

The Board appealed this decision to the Supreme Court, arguing that it was not obliged to reassess the facts before it applied for a permanent injunction as long as it could show that it was in the public interest to prevent the nurse from practising at the time of the first application. The Supreme Court agreed with this argument, but pointed out that a court might not grant the permanent injunction if it was clear that things had changed considerably since granting the interim injunction. Accordingly, the Board must keep up to date with developments so that it can properly decide whether it is worthwhile asking for the injunction to be made final. On the facts, the Supreme Court agreed with the High Court that the injunction should not be renewed or finalised because the circumstances had changed considerably over the intervening two years.

The Supreme Court criticised the Board for dragging the matter on for two years. It pointed out that the Section 44 proceedings were designed to provide speedy relief to the Board whilst the complaints against the nurse were investigated; they were not meant to be used to punish the nurse for two years. The Supreme Court did not go so far as to say that Section 44 imposed a duty on the Board to determine how the situation had changed between the time of the interim injunction and the time of the full hearing, but it made it clear that the court would be reluctant to act on old information. In practice, this should force the Board to complete the disciplinary hearing as soon as possible and to keep up to date with developments between the dates of the first and second hearings.

Section 60 of the Nurses and Midwives Bill 2010 is similar to Section 44 of the 1985 Act. It allows the Board to make an *ex parte* application to suspend a nurse or midwife 'if the Board considers that the suspension is necessary to protect the public until steps or further steps are taken under this Part and, if applicable, Parts 8 and 9'. The application hearing must be in public unless the court decides otherwise. The court can make any appropriate order, including the suspension of the nurse or midwife for a specified period, and it can give the Board any appropriate directions. Given the nature of the Supreme Court's comments about Section 44 of the 1985 Act, which will equally apply to this new section, one must anticipate that if the court does order suspension, it will order a limited period of suspension that will in effect force the Board to gather and present its evidence against the nurse or midwife as soon as it can.

Fitness to practise hearing: summary

1 A nurse can be removed or suspended from the Register of Nurses for misconduct or incapacity.

2 If the Nursing Board decides that removal (erasure) or suspension is too harsh a punishment in the circumstances, the nurse can be restricted or censured.

3 These punishments can be imposed on a nurse only after an inquiry finds him or her guilty of misconduct or incapacitated by reason of physical or mental disability.

4 Section 38 of the Nurses Act 1985 sets out the procedure for the fitness to practise inquiry. Section 44 sets out the procedure where the Board can injunct (legally prevent) a nurse from practising as a nurse before and during the inquiry.

5 This inquiry must obey the principles of natural justice and the nurse must be given a proper opportunity to defend himself or herself against any complaints. The nurse is entitled to expect that the inquiry will be carried out by neutral and impartial people.

6 Section 38 provides for a two-step procedure. First, the Fitness to Practise Committee (FPC) decides whether there is any substance to the complaints made against the nurse. If the FPC and the Board decide that the complaints are serious enough to justify an inquiry, the inquiry will be set up. The nurse must be given a chance to respond to the complaints at the beginning of the first stage, before a decision is made on whether to proceed with the inquiry. In the Nurses and Midwives Bill 2010, each step of this two-step procedure is carried out by a separate committee, namely the Preliminary Proceedings Committee and thereafter the FPC.

7 A nurse is entitled to appeal the decision of the FPC and/or the Board to the High Court.

8 The High Court can disagree with the finding of the FPC and/or the Board and reverse the decision, or it can agree with and confirm the decision, or it can substitute its own decision.

9 It is possible to appeal the decision of the High Court to the Supreme Court, but only on very narrow grounds.

10 The Nurses and Midwives Bill 2010 increases the range of sanctions and measures available to the Board against a nurse or midwife who is found guilty of misconduct. The Bill also provides that all hearings will be held in public, unless the inquiry decides otherwise.

Further reading

'Cases and comment: *O'Ceallaigh* (applicant/appellant) *v Fitness to Practise Committee of An Bord Altranais* (respondents)', *Medico-Legal Journal of Ireland* 7/2 (2001), 90a.

Duffy, G. 'Fitness to practise, preliminary inquiries and fair procedures – a change in standards?', *Irish Law Times* 18 (2000), 298.

Flanagan, J. 'Cases and comment: *Ann O'Ceallaigh* (applicant) *v The Fitness to Practise Committee of An Bord Altranais and An Bord Altranais*', *Medico-Legal Journal of Ireland* 4/2 (1998), 87a.

Nicholas, J. 'Cases and comment: *Ann O'Ceallaigh v An Bord Altranais and Others*', *Medico-Legal Journal of Ireland* 16/1 (2010), 47a.

Useful websites

Ann Kelly support page: http://ireland.iol.ie/~raydj/Ann/entry.htm
'Who Is Ann Kelly?': www.iol.ie/~raydj/Ann/who.htm

chapter 3

THE REGISTERED NURSE PRESCRIBER

Learning outcomes
At the completion of this chapter the reader should know and understand:
- The concept of prescriptive authority.
- The main provisions of the Irish Medicines Board (Miscellaneous Provisions) Act 2006 and the main tenets of the applicable Regulations.
- The role of the Nursing Board.
- The requirements for becoming a registered nurse prescriber (RNP).
- The restrictions placed on an RNP.
- The importance of the collaborative practice agreement.

Prescriptive Authority for Nurses and Midwives

An important development in the professions of nursing and midwifery is that prescriptive authority is no longer the sole domain of the medical practitioner but can now also include a registered nurse prescriber (RNP).

In March 2006 the Minister for Health and Children introduced legislation to allow prescriptive authority for nurses and midwives. The Irish Medicines Board (Miscellaneous Provisions) Act 2006 confers prescriptive authority on nurses and midwives, subject to conditions specified in the Regulations.

In May 2007 the Minister for Health signed into law a network of Regulations:

- Irish Medicines Board (Miscellaneous Provisions) Act 2006 (Commencement) Order 2007.
- Misuse of Drugs (Amendment) Regulations 2007.
- Medicinal Products (Prescription and Control of Supply) (Amendment) Regulations 2007.

These instruments provide the statutory regulatory framework for nurse/midwife prescribing. The professional regulatory framework for nurse/midwife prescribing is established through the Nurses Rules.

Irish Medicines Board (Miscellaneous Provisions) Act 2006

This Act amended existing legislation, primarily Regulations, to make the practice of nurse prescribing legally possible in Ireland. The following Regulations were amended: Medicinal Products (Prescription and Control of Supply) Regulations 2003 and the Misuse of Drugs Regulations 1998 as amended by the Misuse of Drugs (Amendment) Regulations 1993.

The Act is the primary legislation (the bedrock of the law) that allows nurse prescribing, and together with its associated Regulations – Medicinal Products (Prescription and Control of Supply) (Amendment) Regulations 2007, Misuse of Drugs (Amendment) Regulations 2007 and the Nurses Rules – it provides the legislative framework that governs nurse prescribing in Ireland. It is extremely important that nurses know these Regulations well.

Medicinal Products (Prescription and Control of Supply) (Amendment) Regulations 2007

These Regulations set out the statutory requirements for nurse prescribing to occur. They state that a registered nurse prescriber shall not issue a prescription for a medicinal product unless the following conditions are satisfied:

* The nurse is employed by a health service provider in a hospital, nursing home, clinic or other health service setting. It is important to note that the Regulations specifically include the situation where the health service is provided in a private home.
* The medicinal product must be one that would be given in the usual course of treatment provided in the health service setting in which the nurse is employed.
* The prescription is in fact issued in the usual course of the provision of that health service.

In other words, the Regulations envisage the RNP following tried and tested protocols and using familiar products in familiar situations.

The Regulations also make it clear that the health service provider, usually the employer of the RNP, is entitled to restrict a nurse from prescribing a certain medicinal product or to impose conditions (over and above the conditions already set down by law) before that nurse is allowed to prescribe at all. What this means is that even where the RNP has fulfilled the legal requirements necessary for prescribing, his or her employer can impose further conditions (including further qualifications or an experience requirement) before that nurse will be allowed to prescribe whilst rendering services to that employer.

The Regulations specify the information that must be provided by the RNP on the prescription, including the name and the registration number assigned to the nurse in the Register of Nurses established under Section 27 of the Nurses Act 1985.

Misuse of Drugs (Amendment) Regulations 2007

The prescribing of controlled drugs by RNPs is also governed by other Regulations, specifically by Schedule 8 of the Misuse of Drugs (Amendment) Regulations 2007. These amended Regulations identify the drugs that can be prescribed by the RNP and the route of administration for a Schedule 2 or 3 drug prescribed by the RNP. Schedule 8 is divided into three parts, with each part demarcating the prescribing of certain drugs in specified situations. These are detailed later in this chapter.

Nurses Rules

The 'Nurses Rules, 2007' first created a separate division of the Register of Nurses for the RNP. Rule 3(1) of the 'Nurses Rules, 2010' does the same thing. The rules also state that the education programme for nurse prescribers should be in accordance with a curriculum approved by the Nursing Board and carried out in the educational institutions and hospitals approved by the Board for that purpose.

Other sources of regulation and/or information

The Department of Health and the Health Service Executive (HSE) have attempted to supplement (and make more accessible) this complex legislative framework by providing information on an ongoing basis, including guidelines for the role of prescribing site co-ordinators, guidelines for the audit of nurse and midwife prescribing practices, guidelines and policies governing RNPs prescribing in intellectual disability services, guidelines for drugs and therapeutics committees, and the development and use of prescription pads for nurse and midwife prescribers.

The National Nurse and Midwife Prescribing Data Collection System (through the Office of the Nursing Services Director of the HSE) has been activated to monitor the number and type of prescriptions being written by RNPs. This is a huge computerised database and should be accessed by practitioners and prescribers on an ongoing basis.

The Office of the Nursing Services Director of the HSE issued a number of useful publications in 2008 to coincide with RNPs becoming a reality. These are available online from An Bord Altranais (www.nursingboard.ie) and include:

*   *Guiding Framework for the Implementation of Nurse and Midwife Prescribing in Ireland.*
*   *Patient and Service User Information Leaflet.*
*   *Information on Application Guidelines for the Nurse and Midwife Prescribing Initiative.*
*   *Nurse and Midwife Data Collection System.*
*   *An Introduction to the Audit of Nurse and Midwife Prescribing.*

Role of An Bord Altranais

The Nursing Board has three primary functions with regard to nurse prescribing:

*   Professional regulation of RNPs, which primarily involves creating and maintaining a separate division of the Register of Nurses for RNPs.
*   Setting and monitoring minimum standards in the education of RNPs.
*   Guidance and governance of RNPs.

Requirements for Becoming an RNP

It is necessary for a candidate to comply with the *Requirements and Standards for the Education Programme for Nurses and Midwives with Prescriptive Authority* (An Bord Altranais, 2007), which stipulates the minimum requirements for the candidate RNP.

The minimum entry requirements for admission to registration in the Nurse Prescribers Division of the Register of Nurses are:

- Registration as nurse or midwife on the Board's 'live' register.
- Minimum of three years' post-registration clinical experience (within the past five years with at least one year in the area in which prescribing is proposed).
- Possession of competencies recognised at Level 8 on the National Framework of Qualifications.
- Demonstration of continuous professional development and ability to study at Level 8.
- Possession of a competent level of information technology (IT) literacy.

In addition to the above educational requirements, the Board requires a number of other structures to be in place within the health service employer to support the nurse and midwife with prescriptive authority. These are detailed in *Decision-Making Framework for Nurse and Midwife Prescribing* and *Collaborative Practice Agreement (CPA) for Nurses and Midwives with Prescriptive Authority*, which are available online at www.nursingboard.ie. The structures include:

- There must be a local written policy or protocol to support nurse prescribing.
- There must be a collaborative practice agreement (CPA) that supports the nurse prescribing. The CPA is discussed later in this chapter.
- The prescribing must be within the RNP's scope of practice and competency.
- There must have been an assessment of the patient's needs before prescribing.
- The RNP must have sufficient information and skill to determine a treatment plan for the individual patient.
- The RNP must be able to determine the required pharmacological or non-pharmacological treatment option(s) for the patient. If the patient's assessed needs exceed the RNP's scope of practice, the patient must be referred to the appropriate medical practitioner.
- The RNP must initiate the treatment decision only after discussing it with the patient, providing a comprehensive description of the treatment prescribed including expectations of treatment and side effects if any (in other words, a full discussion of the material risks and expected benefits) and agreeing the treatment route with the patient (and/or care giver if applicable).

Registration on candidate register

Whilst the candidate is still a student on the prescribing education programme, he or she needs to submit the 'Application Form for Entry in the Candidate

Register – Post Graduate' no later than thirty days after starting the prescribing education programme. This needs to be done in conjunction with that student's college or university.

Educational qualification

At the time of writing, the School of Nursing, Royal College of Surgeons in Ireland and the Catherine McAuley School of Nursing and Midwifery, University College Cork are providing nurse and midwife prescribing education programmes. These commenced in April 2007. The formal title of the programme is Certificate in Nursing (Nurse/Midwife Prescribing) and the award is at Level 8 (honours level) on the National Framework of Qualifications. The programme, which meets the requirements and standards laid down by the Nursing Board, is being delivered over a six-month period and consists, initially, of twenty-eight days of theory or clinical instruction. There are three core modules:

- Professional accountability in nurse and midwife prescribing.
- Drug action and therapeutics.
- Systemic assessment and evaluation in patient care.

The programme also involves self-directed learning and a twelve-day practical clinical element during which the participating nurse or midwife is supervised by a designated medical practitioner.

Approximately twenty-five students are awarded places per institution per intake. All must meet the following criteria:

- They must obtain support from their health service provider.
- They must satisfy the entry criteria of the higher education institute.
- They must have the support of a medical practitioner, who will act as a mentor for the duration of the programme.
- They must have a minimum of three years' post-registration clinical experience with at least one year in the specific area of practice in which they wish to prescribe.
- The health service employer of the candidate prescriber must have in place, or have access to, a drugs and therapeutics committee and a prescribing site co-ordinator.

On successful completion of the programme, the student is awarded a Certificate in Nursing (Nurse/Midwife Prescribing) and is thereafter entitled to apply to the Board for entry to the Nurse Prescribers Division in the Register of Nurses.

Only applicants who have successfully completed an education programme for prescriptive authority approved by the Board and who are presently employed may apply for registration in the Nurse Prescribers Division. To register, the applicant must submit a completed 'Application Form for Registration in the

Registered Nurse Prescribers Division' and a completed CPA form. Both these forms and a flowchart detailing the registration process can be downloaded from www.nursingboard.ie.

Collaborative Practice Agreement (CPA)

The CPA is drawn up with the agreement of the RNP, the medical practitioner with whom he or she is working, and the employer. It outlines the parameters of the RNP's prescribing authority (i.e. scope of practice). The primary purpose of the CPA is to ensure that the communication and referral mechanisms have been established between the RNP and the medical practitioner regarding the care of their patients and agreed by the employer. Finally, the CPA provides a template for the development, audit and evaluation of the RNP's prescribing practices within the health care setting.

The Nursing Board provides a specific form to be used for the CPA under the 'Registering to Practice – Application Forms' section of its website. A very useful document to read is the *Collaborative Practice Agreement (CPA) for Nurses and Midwives with Prescriptive Authority* (An Bord Altranais, December 2007). This should be read before completing the form as it gives detailed information on the CPA criteria required by the Board. Especially important is the information required on the RNP's practice setting, including the patient/client population and conditions for which the RNP will be responsible. Once again, these documents are available from www.nursingboard.ie.

The RNP Register

Any member of the public can check the register for a nurse's unique personal identification number, a nurse's full name and the divisions in which a nurse is registered. This is an important measure to allow a pharmacist, for example, to check that a nurse is an RNP before dispensing any drugs.

Annual retention fee

To maintain his or her registration with the Nursing Board as a nurse prescriber, the RNP must pay an annual retention fee. Failure to pay this fee will result in the name of the RNP being erased from the Register of Nurses, at least as an RNP. In addition, a nurse prescriber must resubmit a renewed CPA annually.

Change of circumstances

It is very important for an RNP to inform the Nursing Board immediately when he or she changes or leaves a job. An RNP is only authorised to prescribe if employed by a health service provider, as stipulated in the Medicinal Product (Prescription and Control of Supply) (Amendment) Regulations 2007 and the Misuse of Drugs (Amendment) Regulations 2007.

In addition, the 'Nurses Rules, 2010' requires a person whose name is entered in the Nurse Prescribers Division of the Register of Nurses to notify the Board of any change in the name or address of his or her employer or the location of the place of employment. The practical reason for this requirement is that the CPA must be specific to the RNP's current position.

The Board's requirements state that all CPAs are considered null and void on the termination or movement of employment for which the CPA is originally intended. If the RNP leaves his or her current employment or changes the practice area within the current place of employment (for example, if the RNP moves from the Orthopaedic Unit to the Accident and Emergency Department), that RNP must inform the Board in writing within five working days, outlining the reason for this change in status. This notification will have the effect of terminating the existing CPA for that RNP. Thereafter, if the RNP wishes to continue prescribing, he or she will need to fulfil the CPA requirements again for the new practice area. This means that he or she will have to submit a new CPA form to the Board.

Prescription Practice

As discussed earlier, the Medicinal Products (Prescription and Control of Supply) (Amendment) Regulations 2007 stipulate that the following conditions must be met before nurse prescribing can take place:

- The RNP must be employed by a health service provider in a hospital, nursing home, clinic or other health service setting (including a private home).
- The medicinal product must be one that would be given in the usual course of service provided in the health service setting in which the RNP is employed.
- The prescription must be issued in the usual course of the provision of that health service.
- The RNP's An Bord Altranais registration number (also known as the personal identification number or PIN) must be stated on the prescription.

The Regulations do not inhibit the right of an employer to impose further restrictions or conditions.

Drugs an RNP may prescribe

RNPs can prescribe controlled drugs independently, but are subject to specific conditions when it comes to drugs listed in Schedules 2 and 3 of the Misuse of Drugs Regulations 1988. Schedule 8 of the Misuse of Drugs (Amendment) Regulations 2007 outlines the drugs that the RNP may prescribe within Schedules 2 and 3 of the 1988 Regulations. The drugs (and their routes of administration) are set out below.

Part 1: Drugs for pain relief in hospital:
These are drugs prescribed: (I) for the pain relief of a person in a hospital in respect of probable myocardial infarction; (II) for the relief of the acute or severe

pain of a person in a hospital after trauma; or (III) for the post-operative pain relief of a person in a hospital who has had a condition described in (I) or (II).

• Morphine sulphate (oral, intravenous, intramuscular).
• Codeine phosphate (oral).

Part 2: Drugs for palliative care:

• Morphine sulphate (oral, subcutaneous).
• Hydromorphone (oral, subcutaneous).
• Oxycodone (oral, subcutaneous).
• Buprenorphine (transdermal).
• Fentanyl (transmucosal, transdermal).
• Methylphenidate (oral).
• Codeine phosphate (oral).

Part 3: Drugs for the purposes of midwifery:

• Pethidine (intramuscular).

Part 4: Drugs for neonatal care in hospital:

• Morphine sulphate (oral, intravenous).
• Fentanyl (intravenous).

Although the list may be extended in the future, the drugs that an RNP may prescribe are all located within the existing schedules and the law does not allow for nurses to prescribe unlicensed medicines (a medication that has not been approved for licensing or authorisation by the Irish Medicines Board or the European Medicines Agency). See Practice Standard 4 of the *Practice Standards for Nurses and Midwives with Prescriptive Authority* (An Bord Altranais, April 2007).

Registered nurse prescriber: summary

1   The law establishing and regulating the practice of the registered nurse prescriber (RNP) has been in place in Ireland since 2007.
2   There is a separate division in the Register of Nurses for RNPs.
3   There are legal, professional and educational requirements that need to be fulfilled before a nurse or midwife can become an RNP.
4   An employer (health service provider) is entitled to place further restrictions on a qualified RNP, for example requiring specific work experience or stipulating geographical or even situational limitations.
5   The RNP must enter into a collaborative practice agreement (CPA) with the medical practitioner with whom he or she is working, and with his or her employer. This CPA must be renewed and submitted annually to the Nursing Board.
6   The RNP must immediately inform the Nursing Board of any change in circumstance such as leaving a job or altering work location.
7   RNPs can prescribe controlled drugs independently, but are subject to specific conditions when it comes to drugs listed in Schedules 2 and 3 of the Misuse of Drugs Regulations 1988. These conditions are listed in Schedule 8 of the Misuse of Drugs (Amendment) Regulations 2007.

Further reading

An Bord Altranais *Collaborative Practice Agreement (CPA) for Nurses and Midwives with Prescriptive Authority*, Dublin: An Bord Altranais, 2007.

An Bord Altranais *Decision-Making Framework for Nurse and Midwife Prescribing*, Dublin: An Bord Altranais, 2007.

An Bord Altranais *Frequently Asked Questions about Prescriptive Authority for Nurses and Midwives and the Role of An Bord Altranais*, Dublin: An Bord Altranais, 2008.

An Bord Altranais *Guidance to Nurses and Midwives on Medication Management*, Dublin: An Bord Altranais, 2007.

An Bord Altranais *Nurses Rules, 2007*, Dublin: An Bord Altranais, 2007 [repealed by the 2010 Rules but of historical interest].

An Bord Altranais *Nurses Rules, 2010*, Dublin: An Bord Altranais, 2010.

An Bord Altranais *The Introduction of Nurse and Midwife Prescribing in Ireland: An Overview*, Dublin: An Bord Altranais, 2007.

An Bord Altranais and National Council for the Professional Development of Nursing and Midwifery *The Implementation of the Review of Nurses and Midwives in the Prescribing and Administration of Medicinal Products (Final Report)*, Dublin: An Bord Altranais, 2008.

Courtenay, M., Carey, N., James, J., Hills, M. and Roland, J. 'An evaluation of a specialist nurse prescriber on diabetes in-patient service delivery', *Practical Diabetes International* 24/2 (2007), 1–6.

Hickey, G. and Cooper, M. 'The power to prescribe – a new departure for nursing practice', *Medico-Legal Journal of Ireland* 13/1 (2007), 17.

Shannon, J. and O'Riain, S. 'Introduction of "international syringe labelling" in the Republic of Ireland', *Irish Journal of Medical Science* 178 (2009), 291–6.

Useful websites

An Bord Altranais: www.nursingboard.ie

Irish Statute Book: www.irishstatutebook.ie

Part 2

CIVIL
LIABILITY

TORT, BATTERY, AUTONOMY AND CONSENT

> *Learning outcomes*
> At the completion of this chapter the reader should know and understand:
> - What a tort is.
> - The tort of trespass against the person, which includes assault, battery and false imprisonment.
> - The defences to the tort of trespass against the person, the most important of these being consent, but also including necessity or justification.
> - The notion of patient autonomy as an alternative to paternalism.
> - The concept of informed consent.

What Is a Tort and Why Should Nurses Know about It?

A nurse is taught to treat people and save lives. This duty is repeatedly stressed throughout a nurse's training. However, there will be instances where a patient refuses treatment and it is often difficult for a nurse to walk away without doing anything for that patient. This is why nurses need to know about battery, which is the unauthorised touching of somebody, and is one of the oldest torts known in law.

If somebody is harmed or injured whilst in the care of a nurse, then that nurse's performance will be assessed. If it is found to be lacking, there is a chance that the nurse will be judged to be negligent and found liable (responsible) to the injured person for that harm. It is therefore important that nurses understand what is meant by negligence, which is the most well-known of torts.

'Tort' may seem a somewhat exotic and strange sounding word as it is rarely heard in everyday language. The word has Latin origins and was used in the medieval English and French languages, but its use is now limited to the law. It is used to describe a wrong committed by one person against another person, causing personal injury (physiological and/or psychological), physical damage to property or financial loss to that person, which entitles that injured person to be compensated by the person who committed the wrong. It covers situations where a duty that is imposed by law is breached (broken). This is in contrast to the breach of a duty that is imposed by a contract.

The law of torts is a very wide-ranging and diverse area of law. Some of the more well-known torts include negligence, trespass, assault, battery, products liability and intentional infliction of emotional distress. Torts fall into three general categories:

- Intentional torts, for example deliberately hitting a person.

- Negligent torts, for example causing an accident by failing to obey traffic rules.
- Strict liability torts, for example liability for making and selling defective products.

A tort is a civil wrong, as opposed to a criminal wrong, and the usual remedy is damages, which means an amount of money is awarded to the injured party as compensation for their injuries. The person who commits a tort is known as a tortfeasor (wrongdoer) and is the defendant in court.

Please remember that not all actions that result in damage entitle the injured party to sue the person causing the damage. One can only sue if a right that is recognised and protected by law is breached. Where harm results without the violation of a recognised legal right, the injured party is left without a remedy. If I buy a Lotto ticket every week but never win anything, can I sue a Lotto winner on the grounds that they have damaged my chances of winning the Lotto by winning it themselves? Of course not, as I have no right to win the Lotto and it would simply be good fortune if I did. If I go to a sale but fail to get that new jacket I wanted so badly because they have all been purchased already, can I sue the shop for not having a jacket for me, or can I sue the shoppers who purchased the jacket before me and so prevented me from getting one? Again, of course not, as I had no right to the jacket. So it is with the law: I must have a recognised and protected legal right to something before I can sue the person who diminished that right or took it away.

In criminal law it is vital to show the requisite mental element or *mens rea* (guilty mind), which means a person must know that what he or she is doing is a crime. In tort, however, the absence of a malicious motive will not make an otherwise unlawful act lawful. Similarly, the presence of a malicious motive will not normally make an otherwise lawful act unlawful. When speaking of intention in tort, as a general rule it is enough to show that the defendant intended the act or omission that injured the plaintiff, but it is not necessary to show that the defendant intended to injure the plaintiff.

So, for example, if a nurse intentionally lifted a patient out of bed, despite the patient's refusal and protest, and hurt that patient's back, the nurse could be liable as he or she intended to lift the patient out of the bed without consent and it was the lifting that led to the injury. It does not matter that the nurse did not intend to hurt the patient, it is enough to show that the nurse intended to lift the patient out of the bed. The vast majority of wrongdoers in the law of tort did not intend to hurt the person who is suing them; it is their behaviour or conduct that is being measured, not their intentions.

While each individual tort has its own rules governing liability, in most cases a plaintiff must prove that the defendant has infringed a right of the plaintiff that is recognised by law and that some damage was caused to the plaintiff by the tortious act. In some special cases, however, a plaintiff need not prove that there was any damage or loss, merely that his or her legal right was infringed. An example is trespass. These are called torts actionable *per se*, where the wrongful act is penalised, rather than the consequences.

The Tort of Trespass

A defendant can trespass on a plaintiff's land (the most well-known form of trespass); against a plaintiff's goods; or against a plaintiff's person or body, which is the type of trespass examined here. The tort of trespass to the person means direct and intentional acts of interference by the defendant with the person of the plaintiff. It can consist of three acts: assault, battery and false imprisonment. The act that is the cause of the complaint must have been:

- *A voluntary act by the defendant.* In other words, the defendant must have been in conscious control of his or her actions when performing the wrongful or unlawful act that is the cause of the complaint.
- *Intentional.* Unlike criminal law, it is not necessary to show that the defendant intended to injure the plaintiff. When speaking about intention in tort, it is necessary to prove that the defendant intended to commit the act that caused the plaintiff's injury (as opposed to intending to cause the injury itself). In other words, the defendant must be in conscious control of his or her actions, particularly the action that caused the injury.

The plaintiff need not prove that he or she has suffered injury or damages, in the sense of physical or emotional damage, or financial loss. The tort of trespass is a tort actionable *per se*, which means that the wrongful conduct is regarded as being so serious on its own that it must be penalised, even where the damage was minimal or non-existent. However, when the quantum of damages is assessed (i.e. when a monetary value is determined for the compensation amount), then the existence of any damage will be taken into consideration. Finally (and most alarmingly perhaps), unlike other torts, the damages arising from a trespass do not have to be foreseeable – causation is sufficient – otherwise known as damages that 'flow' from the trespass.

It is interesting to note that Section 1(3)(b) of the Courts Act 1988 says that the plaintiff has the right to choose a jury trial in a personal injury action where the action is grounded either in false imprisonment or intentional trespass to the person.

Assault, battery and unlawful imprisonment can also be criminal offences, and this area of law is governed by a statute known as the Non-Fatal Offences Against the Person Act 1997, which will be closely examined in Chapter 12.

The tort of assault

Assault is the threat of or the attempt to apply force to another person that puts that other person in reasonable apprehension that they are about to be 'battered'. In other words, when faced with the conduct of the defendant, an ordinary person would think, 'Uh oh, I'm in for it now!' The shaking of a fist in front of a person's face or the pointing of a loaded gun are assaults, whether or not they are accompanied by threatening words or other gestures, if they cause a reasonable person to think that he or she is about to be the victim of a battery.

It is unlikely that a nurse, or any health professional for that matter, would ever face being sued for assault arising out of his or her professional duties. However, it is possible if the patient could show that he or she was in reasonable apprehension of a contact or impact by reason of the nurse's words or actions. For example, it might be argued that the following words are an assault – 'Stop arguing and sit still so that I can inject you' – if the patient had not consented to the injection and was in reasonable apprehension of having a hypodermic needle plunged into his or her arm.

The tort of battery

Battery is the touching of the person of another, directly (with a part of the defendant's body) or indirectly (with an object under the control of the defendant), however slightly, without the consent of the person being touched. Touching, prodding or rubbing another person without consent are examples of direct battery. Spraying water or detergent over another person, or tipping a bed causing the person to fall out, are examples of indirect battery.

Once again, the unlawful or wrongful act must have been voluntary on the part of the defendant. In other words, the defendant must be in conscious control when committing the act that is the cause of the complaint.

To be successful in an action for battery the plaintiff does not need to prove physical injury. It is sufficient to prove unauthorised contact, which is really touching without permission. A person does not even have to be aware that a battery is being committed upon him or her (for example, if a stranger kisses a sleeping person).

Force is not essential. For example, an uninvited kiss or gentle stroking is a battery. This also explains why it is not necessary for the plaintiff to suffer physical harm or injury, as what is being penalised is the conduct rather than the consequences of that conduct.

The fact that battery can extend to anything that is attached to the plaintiff's body and is practically identified with the plaintiff's body means that it is possible to have indirect battery. It is not necessary to have direct physical contact between the person of the plaintiff and the person of the defendant.

The modern law has effectively done away with the idea that there must be a hostile intent for there to be battery, although it is probably still true to say that one cannot consent to a hostile act of touching.

The tort of false imprisonment

False imprisonment is the unlawful and total restraint of the personal liberty of another. This can be actual physical bondage, whether by manacles or in a cell, or mental bondage, which is achieved by the defendant acting in such a way that the plaintiff knows or reasonably thinks that he or she cannot move.

The essential element is the unlawful detention of a person or the unlawful restraint of his or her liberty. It is not necessary that there be violence or forcible detention. The person does not even have to be aware at the time that he or she is being detained. There must, however, be a total restraint of the liberty of a person. It is not false imprisonment to block a person's way, forcing them to walk around you, although it may be a nuisance.

Again, it is unlikely that a nurse will ever face a claim of unlawful imprisonment, unless he or she straps patients to beds or locks them in the toilet. A nurse might look sternly at a patient who is in the habit of wandering the corridors and say: 'Don't move!', but this would not constitute false imprisonment if the patient was aware that he or she could move if he or she wanted to move. However, if in the same example the patient was a child or a person of diminished capacity and took the words 'Don't move!' to mean he or she was not allowed to move at all, then that could be false imprisonment. The person who uttered those words would have to argue that it was justifiable to order the patient not to move as it is dangerous for patients to be walking freely around the hospital.

Defences to the Tort of Trespass against the Person

Consent

There are two ways of giving consent in Irish law: expressly and impliedly. Express consent is usually oral or written (by word or in writing) and implied consent is usually by conduct (one's behaviour). So, for example, a person impliedly consents to ordinary social contact, such as being bumped in a queue, simply by standing in that queue in the first place. Asking for a haircut is an example of expressly giving consent.

The consent must be given in respect of the actual conduct or act of a substantially similar nature. This raises the question of what exactly patients consent to when they present themselves for treatment. Where consent is pleaded, it must be shown that the terms of the consent were not exceeded. If a patient is admitted for a hernia operation, but the surgeon removes a diseased spleen at the same time on the grounds that it avoided the need for a further and separate procedure, then that would be a battery because consent to a hernia operation can never be 'stretched' to include an organ removal.

The consent must be genuine. Consent obtained by fraud, duress or illegality is not a defence to trespass.

Consent is clearly the most important defence available to the nurse who has been accused of trespass to the patient's person, and is the basis of the notion of informed consent.

Defence of person or property (self-defence)

The defence of person or property is a defence to trespass against the person. To repel force with force is lawful provided that no unreasonable force was used. How much force and of what kind is considered reasonable in the circumstances is a question of fact for the court to decide, but as a rule one does not use a shotgun to defend oneself against a punch. It is to be hoped that a nurse would never have to rely on this defence.

Lawful authority
There are many laws that permit public officials, usually members of An Garda Síochána, to detain or arrest people. As long as the official does not abuse the power conferred, these laws will be a defence to an action for trespass. Similarly, health professionals often act in terms of a statute when treating a patient without consent. An example would be taking blood samples from a person arrested for driving under the influence of alcohol.

Necessity
A person may commit what could be a tort (for example, a battery) to prevent a greater evil from happening and where there is no reasonable alternative. An example would be grabbing somebody by the hair in order to save them from drowning.

Necessity essentially involves the trespass against a person (or a person's property) when that person is not responsible for creating the threat or the need themselves. There must be a threat of 'imminent peril' and the immediacy of that danger leaves one person with no reasonable alternative but to commit the tort on the other person.

It might be argued that the defence of necessity is the legal basis of emergency medicine. The defence of necessity is only available where it is not possible to obtain the patient's consent to treatment and it is reasonable to infer that, where the patient conscious, he or she would have consented to the proposed treatment or procedure. In other words, the concept of necessity cannot be used to override a patient's refusal of treatment when the patient clearly possesses the capacity to refuse.

Patient Autonomy
In instances where the consent of a patient to treatment is not obtained at all, there is clearly a trespass. However, it is not always easy to determine conclusively whether consent was obtained and patients often feel like they have been forced into a decision. It can be a ticklish point as to whether consent has been given at all if it was not given freely.

The relationship between patient and health professional is inherently unequal. This inequality is due to a variety of reasons, including unequal access to knowledge and information, the fact that the patient is often in a state of physical and/or mental weakness, and the natural feelings of dependency that are always present in the treatment relationship.

Although the inequality in power is far more obvious when looking at the relationship between doctor and patient, nurses also have status, knowledge and experience and may appear quite formidable to the patient, who is often vulnerable, dependent and in relative ignorance. Of course, the characteristics of this relationship are found in other professions, for example the relationship of lawyer and client. However, as the medical relationship often involves questions of life and death, privacy and bodily integrity, as well as moral and ethical dilemmas, the law has devoted particular emphasis to it.

Although these questions become far more serious when considering the relationship between doctor and patient, nurses are increasingly being given more authority and responsibility and it is important that these issues of power and inequality are recognised by the nursing profession. In addition, the nurse is often called upon to be a patient advocate. A nurse caught in the middle of a 'power struggle' between the doctor and the patient must be aware of the dynamics of this power relationship and the manner in which the law tries to deal with it.

The law has attempted to correct this power imbalance by developing the concept of patient autonomy, which has been described in a number of ways, including the right of self-governance or the right of self-determination. Essentially the law is concerned here with giving the patient a voice that can be heard and respected. The most important weapon provided to the patient is the patient's power to consent to, or to refuse, any medical treatment. This legal right of the patient is grounded in the Irish Constitution. Article 40.3.1 provides as follows: 'The State guarantees in its laws to respect, and, as far as practicable, by its laws to defend and vindicate the personal rights of the citizen.'

The personal rights of the citizen to consent to, or to refuse, medical treatment as a fundamental personal right is constitutionally protected, provided that the citizen has sufficient mental (intellectual) capacity, sufficient and up-to-date information and freedom of choice (voluntariness). The Supreme Court decision of *In re a Ward of Court* [1996] 2 IR 79 concerned an application to withdraw hydration and nutrition from a patient who, for all intents and purposes, was in a persistent vegetative state. During the course of their respective judgments, Hamilton CJ regarded the right to autonomy as an aspect of the constitutional right of privacy, whilst Denham J regarded autonomy as a separate constitutional right.

In more recent judgments, namely *North Western Health Board v HW & CW* [2001] 3 IR 622, *JM v Board of Management of St Vincent's Hospital* [2003] 1 IR 321 and *Fitzpatrick v FK* [2008] IEHC 104, there seems to be judicial recognition that the right of autonomy is a separate constitutional right, rather than a by-product of privacy.

This line of reasoning has been echoed by the European Court of Human Rights in interpreting Article 8 of the European Convention on Human Rights. The right contained in Article 8 is known as a 'qualified right', as State interference with the rights set out under Article 8 is permissible in certain specific situations. Article 8(1) states: 'Everyone has the right to respect for his private and family life, his home and his correspondence.' This right is subject to the exceptions set out under Article 8(2), which allow these rights to be limited or interfered with in the interests of the permissible aims of the State. Article 8(2) states:

> There shall be no interference by a public authority with the exercise
> of this right except such as is in accordance with the law and is

necessary in a democratic society in the interests of national security, public safety or the economic well-being of the country, for the prevention of disorder or crime, for the protection of health or morals, or for the protection of the rights and freedoms of others.

In its judgment of *Tysiac v Poland* (2007) 45 EHRR 42, the European Court of Human Rights recognised that Article 8 includes the right to personal autonomy. At paragraph 109 of its judgment, the court held:

> The Court also reiterates that 'private life' is a broad term, encompassing, inter alia, aspects of an individual's physical and social identity including the right to personal autonomy, personal development and to establish and develop relationships with other human beings and the outside world. Furthermore, while the Convention does not guarantee as such a right to any specific level of medical care, the Court has previously held that private life includes a person's physical and psychological integrity and that the State is also under a positive obligation to secure to its citizens their right to effective respect for this integrity.

The court's linking of private life with the rights of autonomy and physical and psychological integrity (specifically in relation to medical care) is critically important in the development of the principle of patient autonomy. Similar sentiments were expressed by the same court in paragraph 71 of its judgment in the matter of *Evans v United Kingdom* (2008) 46 EHRR 34.

This emphasis on the polar opposites of paternalism and patient autonomy tends to conceal the practical reality of medical treatment: the concept of collaborative decision making. Rather than looking at medical law as controlling these two opposing forces (nurse/doctor versus patient), some argue that we should be looking at what is often termed 'a therapeutic alliance', which means that the health professional and the patient will consult and agree on what is best for the patient. This sense of shared power, it is argued, will be far more beneficial to the healing process than a situation where the patient is continuously fighting for independence against a health professional who is continuously trying to impose his or her will on the patient.

If the concept of patient autonomy is taken to its extreme it creates an onerous duty on the patient to make all the decisions, relegating the health professional to little more than a bystander awaiting a decision to be made. This seems absurd given that a health professional has a great deal of training and expertise and a patient is more than likely a layperson in the field of medicine. Surely if a medical professional can see that a patient is making the wrong choices for the wrong reasons that professional should be allowed to attempt to persuade the patient to change his or her mind? Can there not be a collaborative thinking process with the autonomy of the patient meaning that the patient makes the final decision after weighing up the options, including the health professional's impassioned arguments?

Irish law does seem to favour a situation where the health professional remains a passive onlooker whilst the patient makes the decision concerning the nature of the treatment or whether there should be any treatment at all. Does this really ensure patient autonomy if the wrong decisions are being made for the wrong reasons, for example if the patient did not really understand the implications of the various options that had been outlined? What is really needed is a relational concept of autonomy rather than a selfish concept of autonomy. The concept of autonomy only makes sense when placed in a social context, much like the African concept of *ubuntu*: we are what others make us.

In addition, as resources become scarcer and patient numbers increase, most doctors simply do not have the time to listen to their patients and cannot enter into mutually beneficial consultations. This is where the role of the nurse should assume greater importance. As doctors are put under increasing pressure, it must become the task of the nurse to listen to patients and to convey their sentiments to the doctor, so that the doctor can consider the thoughts and feelings of each patient.

Similarly, where the nurse can see that a patient does not truly understand the nature or ramifications of the options that the doctor has outlined during the consultation, the nurse needs to step in and ensure that when the patient finally makes the decision, this decision is an informed decision in the true sense. This will protect patient autonomy far more effectively than passively submitting to any decision made by the patient. It is a fine line between collaborating with a patient and unduly influencing a patient, given the power imbalance mentioned earlier, but perhaps the nurse should be providing that equalising force in the doctor–patient relationship.

At the moment the law stands as a referee between two opposing forces, rather than acting as a facilitator between two collaborating parties. By affording nurses an opportunity to learn the law, it is hoped that they will become valuable facilitators in the therapeutic process.

Informed Consent

The concept of informed consent is based on the principle of patient autonomy, indeed, it is really the practical application of that principle. The patient must be in a position to make an educated decision as an expression of free will. This concept originated in medical law, but the phrase 'informed consent' now appears in many other areas of law in recognition of the fact that a person has the right to understand and appreciate the meaning and effect of laws that control their lives.

Consent is one of the common defences. In other words, it is a defence to every tort (within the limits of public decency) that the plaintiff consented to the wrongful actions of the defendant. More specifically, consent is an accepted defence to the tort of trespass against the person.

Informed consent means that the patient agreed to the medical treatment or procedure only after being made aware of the implications of that treatment or procedure, including the risks. This will be examined in far greater detail in Chapters 8, 9 and 10 of this book.

Tort, battery, autonomy and consent: summary

1   Tort is a word used to describe a wrong committed by one person (the defendant) against another person (the plaintiff), causing injury or damage to that person, who is then entitled to be compensated by the person who committed the wrong. If the defendant must compensate the plaintiff, the defendant is said to be liable for the plaintiff's loss or damages.

2   The tort of trespass can be broken down into the three categories: trespass to land, trespass to goods and trespass to the person.

3   Trespass to the person can be broken down into assault, battery and false imprisonment.

4   Medical treatment without any consent is battery.

5   The recognition of patient autonomy means that a patient has the right to accept (consent to) or refuse treatment.

6   Consent is a recognised defence to the tort of battery. The doctrine of informed consent is essentially a modified form of the defence of consent to battery.

7   Necessity or justification is another recognised defence to the tort of battery, where a trespass is necessary to save the plaintiff from more serious harm or 'imminent peril'.

8   Lawful authority is also a recognised defence to the tort of battery. An example would be the taking of a blood sample from an intoxicated driver.

Further reading

Donnelly, M. 'The right of autonomy in Irish law', *Medico-Legal Journal of Ireland* 14/2 (2008), 24–40.

Kelleher, B. 'Medical negligence and MRSA claims: is the law of tort efficient enough?', dissertation, Dublin Institute of Technology, School of Social Science and Law, 2009, posted at http://arrow.dit.ie/aaschssldis/11.

McMahon, S. 'A patient advocate's perspective: consent', *Medico-Legal Journal of Ireland* 14/2 (2008), 62–5.

O'Keefe, S. 'A clinician's perspective: issues of capacity in care', *Medico-Legal Journal of Ireland* 14/2 (2008), 41–50.

Useful websites

British and Irish Legal Information Institute: www.bailii.org
Canadian Journal of Nursing Research: http://digital.library.mcgill.ca/cjnr
Canadian Medical Association Journal: www.cmaj.ca
Irish Student Law Review: www.islr.ie

chapter 5

NEGLIGENCE AND THE DUTY OF CARE

Learning outcomes
At the completion of this chapter the reader should know and understand:
- The legal concept of negligence.
- The elements that need to be proven by a plaintiff who alleges negligence.
- The concept of the duty of care as applied to health professionals.

Negligence

Building on the previous chapter's introduction to the law of tort and in particular the tort of trespass, this chapter focuses on another well-known tort, namely negligence, which is the most common tort. Negligence has a very specific technical meaning and does not mean the same thing as carelessness. When a health provider or health professional is careless it does not automatically follow that he or she will be liable in negligence.

People are negligent in a legal sense when their actions (or lack of action in circumstances where they should have acted) fall short of what is determined as acceptable behaviour and result in a person being harmed in some way. The harm can be a personal injury, physical damage to property or financial loss. The level of care required is expressed as being 'reasonable care in the circumstances'. The difficult part is deciding which circumstances are relevant in a given situation and whether the actions of the defendant, or the skills shown by the defendant, were reasonable or unreasonable. For the most part we look to previous legal decisions and writings for guidance and it is possible to lay down some general principles.

The elements of negligence

The five elements in the tort of negligence are:

- A duty of care was owed.
- There was a failure to conform to the required standard of care (breach of duty).
- Actual loss or damage to the interests of the plaintiff (the patient) occurred.
- There was a sufficiently close causal connection between the conduct of the defendant and the resulting injury to the patient.
- The lack of any defence available to the defendant.

The party alleging the negligence (the patient) must prove the first four elements of negligence in order to succeed in the action.

In some cases the law presumes that the defendant has been negligent when he or she has sole control of the cause of the harm and because the harm could not normally have happened without some element of negligence. The presumption of *res ipsa loquitur* (the facts speak for themselves) is applied in such cases. Note, however, that this is only an evidential presumption. In other words, it is assumed to be the truth unless, and until, a contrary version is proved. The defendant can still lead evidence that provides another plausible reason for the harm caused to the plaintiff.

The Supreme Court ruled in the case of *Lindsay v Mid-Western Health Board* [1993] 2 IR 147 that the principle of *res ipsa loquitur* applied where a person entered hospital for a routine medical procedure and was administered an anaesthetic and subsequently failed to regain consciousness. However, the defendants rebutted (disproved or cast off) the presumption of negligence by proving that all reasonable care and precautions were taken in the administration of the anaesthetic. Accordingly, the plaintiff still had to prove negligence, in the usual way, on a balance of probabilities.

The Duty of Care

As a rule, there is no general duty of care. In other words, there is no general legal duty that says a person must look out for or care for everybody else. In a broad sense, as long as a person is not the creator of the harm, there is no duty of care on that person to save others from that harm.

It was recognised by the courts that there might not be a pre-existing relationship (such as a contract) between a wrongdoer and the victim of that wrongdoing, and that it was necessary to extend the law of negligence to include actions between strangers. The neighbour principle provides that reasonable care must be taken to avoid acts or omissions that can reasonably be foreseen as likely to injure a 'neighbour'. In this case the neighbour is not necessarily the person who lives next door, but rather a neighbour in the wider sense of the word: a person so closely and directly affected by the act or omission that forms the conduct complained of that when the defendant performed that conduct he or she ought to have reasonably contemplated or foreseen that it might cause harm or damage to the person.

In other words, if at the time of doing something (or not doing something I should be doing) I should foresee that what I am doing might harm somebody, I must take steps to avoid harming anybody, pretty much along the lines of the 'look before you leap' principle. Failure to take those reasonable steps to avoid the foreseeable harm amounts to negligent conduct.

Essentially, three requirements need to be established before it can be said that there is a duty of care in existence:

- *Foreseeability.* People owe a duty of care to anyone they can reasonably foresee that they could injure by their acts or omissions.

- *Proximity.* There must be some recognisable or ascertainable connection between the parties. This was often a policy decision, where the court might decide that the existence of a duty of care in a particular situation is just a bad idea for society at large or, conversely, that it is important to create a duty of care between parties where no previous connection had been recognised. In *Glencar Exploration v Mayo County Council* [2002] 1 ILRM 481, the Supreme Court confirmed that the plaintiff needs to prove not only that its loss was foreseeable but also that there was a proximity of relationship between the parties sufficient to justify the imposition of liability. This was in response to some English cases, which had held that a defendant may be liable merely by the fact that the plaintiff proved that his or her losses were reasonably foreseeable. The Supreme Court confirmed that the test is two-tiered: both foreseeability and proximity must be proven by the plaintiff.

- *Just and reasonable.* It must be shown that it is just and reasonable to impose that particular duty of care on the defendant in the circumstances. Again, this often involves a policy decision where the court decides it is necessary to draw a line in order to stop the uncontrolled growth of the duty of care to new areas. It is for this reason that this third limb is somewhat controversial, with many arguing that it is unnecessary and unfair on the plaintiff, who now needs to show that his or her situation is comparable to previous situations where a duty of care was recognised. This would seem to be slowing down the growth of the law, particularly when the second limb already allows the introduction of policy factors including changing the limits of the law when needed.

The duty of care applied to health professionals

A health professional, by virtue of his or her professional relationship with the patient, does owe a duty of care to the patient once that patient has been accepted for treatment. It is sometimes factually problematic whether, or at what stage, a patient has been accepted for treatment, but generally this can be established. Once the relationship is formed, the duty of care that exists in any health care relationship comes into existence as it is readily foreseeable that the negligent conduct of that health professional will cause damage to the patient.

Although some special rules have been formulated to deal with the issue of professional negligence, the primary consideration is whether the health professional exercised the appropriate standard of care and how the court assesses what that appropriate standard of care should be. Apart from that, professional negligence cases are otherwise subject to the ordinary rules on negligence and liability as previously discussed.

As the main focus of any problem involving professional negligence will be how the courts assess what is the appropriate standard of care in any given situation, and the availability of the defence of consistency with approved practice, it is on these areas that we will concentrate in the ensuing chapters.

Negligence and the duty of care: summary

1   Negligence is the most common and well known of the torts.
2   Negligence does not have the same meaning as carelessness. Negligence is a legal concept with a technical meaning.
3   In essence, the concept of negligence is that there is a reasonable standard of conduct for every human situation and a person's conduct is negligent if it falls below that standard.
4   There can be a finding of negligence only if the defendant (the health professional) owes the plaintiff (the patient) a duty of care.
5   In the case of an existing relationship between a health professional and a patient, the question of a duty of care is a given. The query therefore usually relates to whether a sufficient standard of care was practised by the health professional.
6   To succeed in an action for negligence against a health professional, the patient must show: that a duty of care existed between the health professional and the patient; the standard of care expected of that health professional in the circumstances and that the health professional failed to live up to that standard of care; and that the patient suffered damage as a result of the health professional's failure to meet that required standard of care.

Further reading

Byrne, M. 'An overview of recent decisions in the tort of medical negligence', *Medico-Legal Journal of Ireland* 11/1 (2005), 30.
Hunter, S. 'Determination of moral negligence in the context of the undermedication of pain by nurses', *Nursing Ethics* 7 (2000), 379.

Useful websites

Irish Medical News: www.imn.ie
Irish Medical Times: www.imt.ie
Medical Litigation Online: www.medneg.com
Murdoch University Electronic Journal of Law (Australia):
   www.murdoch.edu.au/elaw
Unison: www.unison.org.uk

chapter 6

THE STANDARD OF CARE

Learning outcomes
At the completion of this chapter the reader should know and understand:
- The second element that needs to be proven by the plaintiff alleging negligence, namely the standard of care.
- The legal test of the reasonable person and more specifically the reasonable nurse.
- The approach of the Irish courts in determining the standard of care expected of health professionals.

Introduction

Not long ago the term 'professional negligence' only dealt with the negligent wrongs of a doctor. A distinct division existed between a nurse and a doctor, and the nurse functioned within a much more defined framework. Rather than diagnose patients, treat symptoms or prescribe medication, it was sufficient for the nurse to wait for and then implement a doctor's order, and God forbid that a nurse should criticise that order. The role of the nurse, however, has changed. Today, nurses commonly assume functions previously performed only by doctors, and often perform them without any direct supervision by a doctor. The registered nurse prescriber is an obvious example.

As nursing has matured into an increasingly advanced, sophisticated, specialised and independent profession, the nurse's role in providing patient care has also expanded – a reality that is particularly true in the face of the ever-increasing demand for cost-conscious health care. It must be argued that the result of this development is that when assessing the standard of care expected of a nurse, the methodology used is really the same as that used when assessing the performance of a doctor. What differs is the classification of the standard of care: nurses must be judged against the standard expected of a reasonable nurse in the circumstances under consideration. That is the position that will be adopted in this book and this is an opportune time to discuss why.

In Assessing the Reasonable Standard of Care, Are Nurses 'Professionals'?

When speaking about the standard of care expected of health professionals, we are clearly referring to the profession of medicine and the standard of care expected of a professional in that field. In this work, the term 'health professional' has been used to include both doctors and nurses, and indeed could be used to include others such as dentists and psychiatrists.

'Profession' is defined at www.oxforddictionaries.com as a 'a paid occupation, especially one that involves prolonged training and a formal qualification'. A person is recognised as a qualified and registered nurse only on successful completion of an arduous course of theoretical learning and practical training, and therefore a nurse is clearly a professional as defined. However, an Irish decision is often used as authority for the proposition that nursing is not to be regarded as a profession for the purposes of establishing professional negligence. This decision is *Kelly v St Laurence's Hospital* [1989] ILRM 437.

Facts: Kelly was admitted to the defendant hospital diagnosed with epilepsy. He had been acting rather strangely and the reason for his admission to the hospital was to determine whether this behaviour was as a result of epilepsy or as a result of schizophrenia. Kelly was taken off all medication as a necessary prerequisite to his diagnosis. Some nights after his admission, Kelly left the ward, climbed onto a windowsill in a nearby toilet and fell some twenty feet into a yard below, severely injuring himself. The jury found that the hospital was negligent in allowing the patient to go to the toilet unaccompanied, given his history. The hospital appealed this decision, saying that there was no evidence of negligence.

Issue before the court: Was the accident reasonably foreseeable?

Decision of the court: The court dismissed the appeal (i.e. it found against the hospital) and held that the duty of care owed to the patient was for the hospital to take reasonable care to avoid permitting him to be exposed to injury that a reasonable person ought to foresee.

The parts of the reported judgment that form the basis of the proposition that nurses are not to be regarded as professionals for the purpose of establishing clinical negligence are set out below.

Finlay CJ said:

> I am satisfied, however, that as appears from the form of the question left to the jury, the propriety of which is not challenged, that this is more precisely a case where the issue is one of nursing care and attention than it is of one where the allegation of negligence is to be categorised as negligence in medical treatment. Undoubtedly, the extent and nature of the care and attention which a reasonably careful hospital would have afforded to the plaintiff whilst he was an in-patient there on 15 July 1981 and in particular, of course, the question as to whether a reasonably careful hospital staff would have arranged for a person to attend him when he left the ward in the middle of the night to go to the toilet, depends to a very large extent on the foreseeability from a medical point of view of the risk that the plaintiff would, if allowed to go unattended to the toilet in the middle of the night, injure himself in some way.
>
> That does not, however, seem to me to make this a case solely to be tested by the standards which have been accepted by the courts with

regard to allegations of negligence in treatment afforded to their patients by professional medical people.

And Walsh J added:

> What was in issue in this case was not a question of medical negligence in the strict sense as arose in the case of *O'Donovan v Cork County Council*. What was in issue was the adequacy of the system and of care for the plaintiff by the hospital authorities while he was in their hospital. There is no question of any allegation of negligence against the consultant who treated the plaintiff while he was in hospital. It is also clear from the evidence given by the consultant that he, in effect, was distancing himself from any responsibility for the way the nurses in question and the rest of the nursing staff carried out their duties, and, as he pointed out in his evidence, in effect, that it was up to them to know their patient and to give him the care appropriate to his condition and his case history and, above all, appropriate to the reason why he was in the ward in question.

Perhaps the easiest way to understand this judgment is to look at the policy behind it. It must be remembered that professional negligence is a subset of the ordinary rules of negligence, with most issues concentrated on the question of the appropriate standard of care.

Traditionally the courts restricted the 'professions' to lawyers, doctors and clergy. The courts' approach to these professions seemed to be based on two premises that combined to make the task of the plaintiff very difficult if the defendant was a member of one of these professions. First, the reputation of a professional was an extremely valued and valuable entity and the courts would not lightly attack it. Second, medical professionals possessed qualifications and skills that were not easily understood by a person not qualified to practise medicine (and this included judges) and therefore the opinions of these professionals had to be treated with deference, unless they were obviously out of kilter with the rest of their profession. The judge (and juries) at that time relied on medical expert witnesses to analyse issues of fact and draw inferences from the evidence of a specific practice.

If it is recognised that the rules of law pertaining to professional negligence (as opposed to ordinary or simple negligence) are strongly biased in favour of the defendant, then patient advocates might argue that the fewer practitioners covered by the 'professional' cloak of protection the better. And it is perhaps to this that the judges were referring. When using the term 'professional', they were using it not in the popular sense of somebody in a profession, but rather to refer to somebody who is protected by the special rules and laws that the courts have formulated over the years to protect the defendant's professional reputation. Accordingly, from a legal point of view, nurses will be tested by the ordinary rules of negligence, even though the modern nurse is highly qualified and undertakes many of the tasks previously done only by doctors. This is a legal policy approach, where the courts are trying to level the playing field between plaintiff and defendant. It must not be seen as a slight on the nursing profession.

Judges may be less deferential to expert opinion today and this distinction may not make that much of a difference as a nurse's performance will be judged against that of the reasonable nurse with his or her qualifications and experience. The term 'ordinary negligence' cannot be taken to mean that a nurse will be assessed according to the standards of an ordinary person without any special skills. Such an approach would be illogical and would make the plaintiff's task even more onerous, which is what the courts are trying to avoid.

It must rather be argued that although both doctors and nurses are health professionals in the ordinary sense of the word, they have different qualifications and different duties and hence the duty of care is different. This is in effect the subjective element in an otherwise objective test. A nurse will be assessed against the standard of a reasonable skilled nurse, and a doctor against the standard of a reasonable skilled doctor. This is hardly a ground for saying that a nurse is not a professional whereas a doctor is. It is instead acknowledging that their professions are different and therefore their duties of care are different.

This was the approach adopted by the High Court in the case of *Healy (a minor) v HSE and Fitzsimons* [2009] IEHC 221.

Facts: Paul Healy was born in Tralee General Hospital on 14 February 2000. The birth was satisfactory and the baby appeared to be perfectly healthy at birth. However, his mother had a lot of trouble feeding him, he was unsettled and he cried continuously. The baby vomited 'a dirty yellow and green coloured vomit' two days after his birth. The duty nurse at the time described the vomit as an 'egg-yolk yellow, curdy-coloured fluid'. Paul's mother repeatedly voiced her concerns to the nursing staff and even brought the baby's stained clothing to the nurses' station on a number of occasions. She asked the nurses to show the clothing to Dr Robert Fitzsimons, who was the consultant paediatrician responsible for Paul's care. Fitzsimons was informed by the nurses of the vomiting and he instructed them to observe the child and to undertake a midstream urinalysis.

The Healys were discharged from hospital three days after the birth, with the attendant doctor giving both mother and child a clean bill of health. However, Paul's condition did not improve and he was brought back to the hospital by his parents and readmitted four days after his birth, on 18 February 2000. An acute bowel obstruction was diagnosed and he was transferred by ambulance to Our Lady's Hospital in Crumlin, where surgery disclosed an intestinal malrotation and a small-bowel volvulus. The staff in Crumlin gave Paul little chance of survival.

Paul did survive, but had to remain in hospital for over seven months, during which time he underwent extensive and serious surgeries, including five laparotomies. He had repeated small-bowel resections, after which less than one per cent of his small bowel remained.

Through his mother, Paul sued the Health Service Executive (HSE) and

Dr Fitzsimons for damages, claiming his injuries were caused by their negligence and breach of duty. The plaintiff's case essentially rested on the argument that when Paul exhibited the classic symptoms of malrotation, he should have been treated by the defendants as a surgical emergency. It was alleged that the defendants failed to recognise those symptoms and wrongly discharged Paul from the hospital three days after his birth, when they should have been surgically correcting the malrotation and thereby avoiding the occurrence of a volvulus — a twisting of the intestine that happens because it is not secured, or is inadequately secured, to the abdominal wall. This twisting of the intestine will prevent or obstruct the path of nutrients through the intestinal tract. It also results in intestinal obstruction and ischaemia due to the interruption of the blood supply to the intestine. The intestinal obstruction causes bile to pour into the intestine, which results in bile-stained vomit, a classic symptom of volvulus. Ischaemia results in necrosis of the affected part of the bowel, which then becomes gangrenous. The resulting condition is known as necrotising enterocolitis.

Evidence was led that the consequences of Paul's injury were 'permanent and catastrophic'. Upon his discharge from Crumlin hospital he required continuous intensive care, including intravenous feeding, in a totally sterile environment that had to be artificially created in his home. His need for constant care meant that both his parents had to give up their jobs to stay at home with him. His condition was likely to remain serious throughout his life, severely diminishing his chances of earning income or having a career.

Issue before the court: When the trial was in its ninth day, the defendants conceded that they had been negligent and were responsible for Paul's injuries. Accordingly, the issue before the court was the extent of the defendants' respective liability.

Decision of the court: The court found that on being informed that the baby had vomited yellow-coloured fluid at least twice on 16 February 2000, Dr Fitzsimons should have immediately referred the baby for investigation, either by way of a barium meal X-ray or by a paediatric surgeon. His decision merely to continue observation of the baby was below the standard required of a consultant paediatrician and his failure to refer the baby for a surgical opinion or an X-ray was negligent and in breach of his duty to Paul.

The judge also criticised the nursing staff at Tralee hospital. He found that they did not investigate Mrs Healy's concerns with sufficient efficiency or urgency and did not adequately monitor and record the occurrence and number of the baby's bile-stained vomits on 16 February. This failure meant that they too fell below the standard of care expected of a nursing staff at a general hospital and so they were negligent and in breach of their duty to Paul.

Finally, the decision to discharge Paul when both medical and nursing staff had not taken steps to ascertain that his bile-stained vomits had not been caused by reason of malrotation and volvulus was again a fundamental breach of their duty of care to their patient.

The court found that both defendants were liable for Paul's injuries and therefore both had to pay him damages, with 75 per cent to be paid by the consultant and 25 per cent to be paid by the hospital.

Throughout his judgment, Quirke J made it clear that the consultant and the nursing staff had distinct duties of care towards the patient, which they had failed to discharge:

> The advice given by the nursing staff when Mrs. Healy telephoned on 17th February, was inappropriate and incorrect. By failing to direct Mrs. Healy to return with the plaintiff immediately to the hospital, the nursing staff within the hospital failed to adopt and apply general and approved medical practice and were negligent and in breach of their duty of care to the plaintiff. [. . .]
>
> The members of the nursing and medical staff of the hospital were in serious breach of their duty to the plaintiff when they discharged him from hospital on 17th February, 2000. They were also in serious breach of their duty of care to the plaintiff subsequently on 17th February, 2000, when they gave his mother entirely inappropriate advice and instructions when she telephoned the hospital on three separate occasions. [. . .]
>
> The plaintiff would not have suffered his injury if the nursing and medical staff of the hospital had not failed to discharge their *separate and independent duty of care* [my italics] to the plaintiff on the evening of 16th February, 2000, and during 17th February, 2000. They failed repeatedly to discharge that duty during that time. [. . .]
>
> Although imperilled by the negligence of Dr. Fitzsimons, the plaintiff was *independently entitled* [my italics] to appropriate care and medical treatment from the hospital's nursing and medical staff on the evening and night of the 16th February, and during 17th February, 2000. [. . .]
>
> If he had received the standard of care and medical treatment to which he was entitled from the nursing and medical staff, then he would not have been discharged from hospital on 17th February, 2000, and, as a matter of probability, his mother would not have been given inappropriate advice and he would have been referred for surgical investigation no later than 17th February, 2000. [. . .]
>
> In consequence, he would not, as a matter of probability, have developed necrotising enterocolitis and have suffered the catastrophic consequences which followed.

This decision makes it clear that each professional person – nurse, doctor or consultant – has a duty of care that must satisfy a particular standard expected of that person. That duty, and the standard exacted by the duty, is independent of any other standard or duty of care owed by any other professional. Accordingly, titles such as 'professional' are, from a legal point of view, more descriptive than determinative.

The courts are moving away from the traditional position of deferring to the 'professions' – doctors, lawyers and clerics – and ultimately the decision as to whether a standard of care was achieved is a legal question to be answered by the court, perhaps using ordinary principles of negligence law rather than being decided by the profession of which the defendant is part.

Care must be taken in assessing the standard expected of a professional and must take into account the skills he or she claims to hold to avoid demanding unrealistic standards of skill and knowledge. A general practitioner consulted by a patient complaining of stomach ache is not expected to have the same level of knowledge and expertise as a consultant gastro-enterologist, but as a reasonable general practitioner he or she should know when it is time to refer the patient to the specialist consultant. Similarly, a nurse who is a specialist theatre nurse will be assessed against that standard, as will a nurse who is a specialist accident and emergency nurse. They are all 'professionals'; they just have different qualifications and responsibilities and thus the standard of care expected of them will be different.

As previously mentioned, whilst this certainly has a subjective element to it, it is an objective test. The standard of care achieved by a particular person with a particular qualification will be measured against the standard of care expected of the reasonable professional with the same skills or qualifications.

Reaching, or Breaching, the Required Standard of Care

When talking about a breach of a duty of care, we are actually covering two issues: the content of the duty of care and whether the defendant discharged that duty of care. The first matter is legal in nature, the second is factual. Put simply, if we recognise that a duty of care is owed by one person to another person, we must determine just how good that care must be. This measure of care is called the standard of care. Once this standard is determined, we must look at the facts and ask whether the defendant has measured up to this standard. The usual standard of care recognised by the law is that of the reasonable person.

In the case of *Kirby v Burke* [1944] IR 207, the test in regard to a reasonable person was stated as follows:

> . . . the foundation of liability at common law for tort is blameworthiness as determined by the average standards of the community; a man fails at his peril to conform to these standards. Therefore, while loss from an accident generally lies where it falls, a defendant cannot plead an accident if, treated as a man of ordinary intelligence and foresight, he ought to have foreseen the danger which caused injury to his plaintiff.

The reasonable person is a fictitious person who represents a standard of conduct that must be regarded as a goal to be worked towards. It is an objective standard or measurement of conduct, against which the actual conduct of the defendant is compared. It is like describing and explaining the surrounding circumstances to 'the average person in the street' and then asking whether he or she thinks that the defendant's performance was acceptable – a sort of 'opinion poll of performance'.

A reasonable person is expected to know the facts of common experience and the laws of nature. A reasonable person is expected to know and appreciate his or her personal limitations and to act accordingly. That objective standard of behaviour is raised where a person possesses or claims to possess special skills or qualifications. As noted above, this introduces an element of subjectivity into an objective test as the performance of that person with skills or qualifications will be measured against that of a reasonable person with those skills or qualifications.

The Reasonable Nurse

The question posed asks whether a defendant nurse (whose actions or inactions are being examined) exercised the appropriate standard of care expected of a reasonable nurse. In other words, did the nurse practise the degree of skill that a member of the public would expect from a person in his or her position?

One must also remember that as the magnitude of the risk increases so does the level of precaution required by the defendant. The magnitude of the risk, in turn, is affected by the likelihood of injury occurring and the extent of the threatened harm. This is important in the field of medicine where decisions made often carry a high degree of risk and accordingly a high standard of care will be imposed.

In the Irish decision of *Kelly v Governors of St Laurence's Hospital* [1988] IR 402 at 415, Henchy J clarified the relationship between the likelihood of harm occurring and the required standard of care: 'In my view the essential question is whether the risk of injury or damage complained of was such that a reasonably careful person in the position of the defendant would have taken the precaution suggested by the plaintiff.'

Three specific areas of a health professional's work are often being examined when looking at the law of negligence: diagnosis, treatment and disclosure (of material risk). The first and the third are primarily within the professional responsibility of the doctor rather than the nurse, but the question of whether the nurse has met the required standard of treatment must be examined.

As a starting point in deciding what is a reasonable standard of care, the court will be guided, but not ordered, by comparable nurses and what those nurses view as a 'general and approved practice'. This concept was explained by the Supreme Court in the case of *O'Donovan v Cork County Council* [1967] IR 173:

> A medical practitioner cannot be held negligent if he follows general and approved practice in the situation with which he is faced . . . That proposition is not, however, without qualification. If there is a common practice which has inherent defects, which ought to be obvious to any person giving the matter due consideration, the fact that it is shown to have been widely and generally adopted over a period of time does not make the practice any the less negligent.

Neglect of duty does not cease by repetition to be neglect of duty. Furthermore, if there be a dispute of fact as to whether or not a particular practice is a general and approved practice, it is a matter for the jury to determine whether or not the impugned treatment is general and approved practice.

The test is whether the standard of care followed general and approved practice within the profession. Would another nurse of similar skill and qualification have done the same thing or followed the same approach? However, where a nurse adopts a practice that, in the opinion of the court, contains clear defects, then it is not a defence that the defective practice was practised by other nurses of similar skill and qualification.

It is a legal question, and not a medical question, as to whether the nurse exercised the requisite standard of care. Clearly the court will be guided, but not ruled, by what other members of the nursing profession would regard as a general and approved practice. The general and approved practice defence will fail if a reasonable nurse should have spotted an inherent defect in that established practice if he or she had bothered to examine that practice properly.

This approach was confirmed in the case of *William Dunne (an infant suing by his mother and next friend Catherine Dunne) v The National Maternity Hospital and Reginald Jackson* [1989] IR 91, where the Supreme Court held:

- In considering whether a doctor's diagnosis and treatment were negligent, a finding of negligence would be made only if it was shown that no practitioner of equal status and skill, acting with ordinary care, would have done the same.
- A deviation from a general and approved practice will be negligent unless another doctor of equal status and skill, acting with ordinary care, would have done the same.
- It is not a defence for a doctor to claim that he or she followed an established practice of conduct if the practice has inherent defects that should be obvious to any person who carefully considered the procedure.
- Where there is an honest difference of opinion between two doctors as to which is the better procedure or treatment to follow, this difference of opinion does not provide any ground for leaving a question to the jury as to whether the defendant who has followed one course rather than the other has been negligent. It is not for the judge or jury to decide which of the two courses was better, but rather whether the course that was followed complied with the careful conduct of a medical practitioner of like specialisation and skill as that of the defendant.
- Where there is a dispute of fact as to whether the practice in question is or is not general or approved, that question must be left for the decision of the jury.
- For a practice (be it treatment or diagnosis) to be regarded as general and approved, it does not have to be followed by everybody but must be an

approved procedure that is followed by a substantial number of reputable practitioners holding the relevant specialist or general qualifications.

The court explained these principles as follows:

> In order to fully understand these principles and their application to any particular set of facts, it is, I believe, helpful to set out certain broad parameters which would appear to underline their establishment. The development of medical science and the supreme importance of that development to humanity makes it particularly undesirable and inconsistent with the common good that doctors should be obliged to carry out their professional duties under frequent threat of unsustainable legal claims. The complete dependence of patients on the skill and care of their medical attendants and the gravity from their point of view of a failure in such care, makes it undesirable and unjustifiable to accept as a matter of law a lax or permissive standard of care for the purpose of assessing what is and is not medical negligence. In developing the legal principles outlined and in applying them to the facts of each individual case, the courts must constantly seek to give equal regard to both of these considerations.

The Supreme Court was taking the decision away from the expert witnesses, back to where that power of decision belongs, with the court itself: a judgment of court is a legal decision, not a medical decision. This is accepted practice in other areas of law, where it is recognised that an expert witness is giving an opinion, as opposed to factual evidence, and therefore this opinion can be rejected by the judge if considered illogical or fanciful. It would seem that the medical profession is finally being treated like other professions with regard to expert witnesses. Having said that, in practice, the court must rely on expert witnesses to form opinions and judgments on complex scientific issues and draw inferences from evidence of professional practices. The court must remain in control of the process by applying common sense to conflicting theories and arrive at conclusions as to what probably happened.

This approach has been more recently followed by Irish courts in *Collins v Mid-Western Health Board* [2000] 2 IR 154, *Griffin v Patton* (Unreported, SC, 27 July 2004) and *Shuitt v Mylotte* [2006] IEHC 89.

Whilst it must be conceded that the courts cannot really adopt any other approach when it comes to the issues of diagnosis and treatment, it could perhaps be argued that the ordinary rules of negligence and the duty of care should be applied to the question of disclosure of material risks, including whether materiality should be decided by the health professional or the patient. This issue will be examined in Chapter 9.

There is another consequence of this approach. If the conduct of the defendant must be shown to be logical and reasonable, it does not follow that simply failing to observe the accepted practice is in itself evidence of negligence, since there might be very strong reasons for the defendant's decision not to follow standard procedure in that case. Where a decision has been made carefully and with great consideration, seems reasonable and logical and is supported by substantial professional opinion, even if not everyone would have followed the same practice, it is doubtful that the court would find negligence. There must be room for difference in opinion, as long as that opinion was reasonable in the circumstances.

The court will only be guided by professional opinion where that opinion is shown to be reasonable and logical in the circumstances, perhaps even where the decision made flew in the face of established opinion. A science develops and progresses by testing the 'tried and trusted'. This might very well apply to a nurse, who may be told to do something a certain way for no other reason than 'it has always been done that way'. If a nurse comes to a considered decision that there is a better way to do that thing, the law will not necessarily shoot him or her down for thinking along new lines, as long as the nurse's thought process is logical and reasonable and supported by previous experience.

Accordingly, the law regarding standard of care can be stated as follows:

- There is no breach of the standard of care if the nurse has acted in accordance with the practice accepted as proper by a responsible body of professional skill in the nursing profession, and this practice was appropriate (i.e. reasonable and logical) in the circumstances of the case.
- There is no breach of the standard of care if there is no acceptable body of opinion covering the situation at hand, but what the nurse did was considered reasonable and logical in all the circumstances.
- There is no breach of the standard of care if the nurse did not follow the accepted practice, but his or her actions were reasonable and logical in all the circumstances and would be supported by competent professional opinion.
- On the question of foreseeability, the law recognises that precautions can be taken against only reasonably known risks. If a risk is not known at the time, precautions cannot be taken against an unforeseeable possibility. However, once that risk is known, the standard of care increases as the defendant is expected to know of the risk.
- Nurses must ensure that they are always aware of standing instructions and accepted codes of practice as these often contain the latest information on accepted procedure. A failure to follow a standing instruction or code of practice without some exceptional justification would usually mean negligence.

Standard of care: summary

1   The common law general standard of care is described as the standard of care expected of the 'ordinary person'. This is an objective test and represents a goal to be worked towards. Persons holding themselves out to the public as having specific skills or qualities, or belonging to a particular profession, must exercise the standard of care that a reasonable member of the public is entitled to expect from somebody with those qualifications or belonging to that profession. A nurse is expected to exercise the skills of a reasonable qualified nurse; a general practitioner is expected to exercise the skills of a reasonable qualified GP; and a specialist practitioner is expected to exercise the skills of a reasonable specialist in his or her field.

2   A nurse will be negligent if no nurse of equal status and skill, acting with ordinary care, would have done the same.

3   It is not a defence for a nurse to argue that he or she followed an established practice if the practice has inherent defects that should be obvious to any person giving due and proper consideration to the matter.

Further reading

Mustard, L. W. 'Caring and competency', *JONA's Healthcare Law, Ethics, and Regulation* 4/2 (2002), 36–43.

Tingle, J. 'Commentary on Young A', *Journal of Clinical Nursing* 19/1 (2010), 297–9.

Weld, K. K. and Garmon, S. C. 'Concept analysis: malpractice and modern-day nursing practice', *Nursing Forum* 44/1 (2009), 2–10.

Young, A. 'The legal duty of care for nurses and other health professionals', *Journal of Clinical Nursing* 18/22 (2009), 3071–8.

Useful websites

Irish Nurses and Midwives Organisation: www.inmo.ie

Nurses.info: www.nurses.info

Nursing Standard: http://nursingstandard.rcnpublishing.co.uk

'Quality of Nursing Care': www.ciap.health.nsw.gov.au/hospolic/stvincents/1992/a04.html

DAMAGES AND CAUSATION

> *Learning outcomes*
> At the completion of this chapter the reader should know and understand:
> - The third element that needs to be proven by the plaintiff alleging negligence, namely that the plaintiff has suffered damages.
> - The computation of damages by the court.
> - The fourth element that needs to be proven by the plaintiff alleging negligence, namely that the damages suffered were caused by the defendant.
> - The concepts of factual causation and legal causation and the approach of the Irish courts in this regard.
> - The impact of the Civil Liability Act 1961.

Damages

In essence, when one speaks about damages in medical law, and in the law of tort in general, one is talking about compensation, which in turn means money. The principle underlying the concept of damages is restitution; in other words, to place the plaintiff in the position they would have been in if the tort had not happened. This is usually impossible in medical negligence cases as the patient, for example, may have lost a limb or will be in poor health for the rest of his or her life. The court can therefore only try to compensate the patient as best it can.

Many would argue that money can never undo the wrong suffered by a patient at the hands of a health care professional. Others argue that the lure of money often causes patients to sue health care professionals for the wrong reasons. Neither of these arguments is totally right or totally wrong. For both parties, litigation is highly stressful and expensive. It is difficult for a court to deal with the hurt and anger felt by wronged patients in any other way than by compensating them. By their very nature and function courts are not equipped to offer solace or holistic healing, and they do not pretend to do so.

It must also be recognised that money awards can lead to greed and less than honourable behaviour on the part of patients, who can pressurise a health professional merely by threatening to sue or 'go public'. This is turn leads the health professional to practise safe or defensive medicine, which may stultify progress, and to take out very expensive insurance policies, the expense of which is passed on to patients in the form of higher fees.

No-fault compensation

A possible solution to the problems associated with fault liability and medical malpractice litigation is the concept of no-fault compensation, where the patient does not need to show that a health professional or hospital is at fault. What the plaintiff needs to show is that he or she suffered damages as a result of medical treatment. In other words, causation must be established but not fault. Two countries that have introduced no-fault compensation systems are New Zealand and Sweden.

Ireland has the Personal Injuries Assessment Board (PIAB) but medical negligence claims have been expressly excluded from its jurisdiction.

Calculation or Computation of Compensatory Damages

When the plaintiff claims compensatory damages for personal injury, these damages are assessed under the headings of special or pecuniary damages, general or non-pecuniary damages, and occasionally aggravated damages.

Special damages or pecuniary damages are those damages that it is possible to compute because of their monetary nature. Examples would include:

- Medical expenses such as the cost of the hospital bills, a doctor's fee, medications, rehabilitation training and any miscellaneous medical costs.
- Loss of wages, both in the past and in the future if the plaintiff is unable to go back to work in his or her previous job or at all. These damages are often assessed or computed by an actuary, who is called as an expert witness.

In practice, these figures are often agreed beforehand and are not challenged in court. This is as a result of the difference between liquidated damages and unliquidated damages. Liquidated damages are damages that can be calculated exactly, and therefore can be agreed between the parties to a dispute. If they come to an agreement on a specific figure, then all that needs to be done is for the parties to inform the court what that agreed figure is. Unliquidated damages are not capable of exact calculation (and are sometimes referred to as 'thumb-suck damages' for obvious reasons). Where the parties cannot agree on a sum or where it is not possible to calculate an exact sum, then it is the task of the court to decide on a figure.

As a general rule, special damages (for example, medical expenses, loss of wages) are liquidated damages, and general damages (for example, pain and suffering) are unliquidated damages.

A plaintiff is paid general damages for pain and suffering to the date of his or her court hearing and for any future pain and suffering or for any loss of amenity that he or she suffers. These are called general damages as it is impossible to calculate an exact figure, and this amount is decided by the court. The court must attempt to predict the future and make provision for what the plaintiff will need, perhaps for the rest of his or her life. This is an extremely complex task and the court is guided by experts such as actuaries who are qualified to make these calculations. When it comes to general damages, which cannot be calculated, the court will look at previous decisions, taking into account factors such as inflation and the cost of living.

Aggravated damages can be awarded to compensate the plaintiff for harm suffered due to the behaviour of the defendant. Factors the court will take into account are:

- The manner in which the wrong was committed. For example, was it accompanied by oppressive or aggressive behaviour?
- The conduct of the defendant after the wrong was committed. For example, was there an apology or a threat?
- The conduct of the defendant or his or her representative in the period pending litigation. For example, was there a genuine attempt to settle the matter in an amicable fashion or was there an abuse of the pre-trial process?

By way of an example, in *Philp v Ryan* [2004] IESC 105, which was a medical negligence action, the court made an award of aggravated damages against the defendant, a medical doctor, of €50,000, when it was shown that he had falsified his notes.

Causation

The plaintiff (the patient) needs to show that there is a causal link between the harm suffered by the patient and the failure of the defendant (the health service provider) to follow the approved practice or procedure. Picture in your mind a chain connecting the act or omission of the defendant to the harm or injury caused to the plaintiff. If that chain is unbroken, causation is established.

There are essentially two tests for causation: the actual causation test (often called factual causation or cause in fact) and the legal causation test (often called proximate cause). One must not read this to mean that the actual causation test does not involve questions of law or that the legal causation test does not involve questions of fact. These two tests are not mutually exclusive, but should rather be seen as complementing each other. However, where the facts are such that the courts can determine causation using the factual test, they will not have recourse to the legal causation test. Unfortunately, the nature of medical negligence cases is that often the factual test is not sufficient to analyse properly the facts concerning who did what or to what extent, and the development of the legal causation test has largely been due to medical negligence cases.

Actual causation

The actual causation or factual causation test is the easier of the two to understand and apply. It relies primarily on evidence of fact and essentially it asks one question: was the defendant's negligent act the factual cause of the plaintiff's harm?

The 'but for' test

The traditional approach to the factual causation test is to use the 'but for' test. But for the defendant doing what he or she did, would the harm have occurred?

An English decision that clearly illustrates this approach in the clinical field is *Barnett v Chelsea Kensington Management Committee* [1968] 1 All ER 1068.

Facts: The deceased drank a cup of tea and felt ill. He went to hospital where he was treated by a nurse who consulted with a doctor over the telephone. After being treated, the deceased left the hospital. He died soon after. It was discovered that the cup of tea had contained arsenic and the deceased had died of arsenic poisoning. Evidence was led and accepted by the court that cases of arsenic poisoning were rare and that even if the deceased had been admitted to the hospital and treated, there was little or no chance that an effective antidote would have been administered to him in time to save his life.

Issue before the court: Was the doctor negligent in not physically examining the patient instead of consulting over the telephone? And if so, was the hospital liable for the harm suffered by the plaintiff, the deceased's widow, arising from his death?

Decision of the court: The court found that the doctor had indeed been negligent in not seeing the deceased patient personally. However, the court went on to find that the deceased was in any event doomed to die and the fact that the doctor did not see him personally did not cause his death. Therefore the harm was not 'but for the doctor's negligence' and there was no causal link.

An Irish case that adopted the reasoning of the *Barnett* decision was *Kenny v O'Rourke* [1972] IR 339.

Facts: The plaintiff fell off a ladder and was seriously injured. Evidence was led that the ladder was defective. This evidence was countered by evidence for the defendant that the plaintiff was leaning too far out on the ladder and this caused the ladder to topple.

Issue before the court: Should the defendant be held liable for supplying a defective ladder, where it would seem that the conduct of the plaintiff, rather than the defective ladder, was the ultimate cause of the injury?

Decision of the court: On the evidence, the injury was due to the plaintiff's leaning too far over rather than the defective ladder. By using the 'but for' test it could not be said that but for the defect in the ladder the plaintiff would not have been injured.

Although the 'but for' test is appealing in its logic and simplicity, the mechanical and unfeeling nature of the test can lead to difficulties. Decisions by the court based on this test might be regarded as unfair by the ordinary person, particularly in circumstances where that ordinary person thinks that the health professional should be held liable. For example, if the average person was asked about the arsenic tea case, his or her response would be along the lines that the doctor did not do a proper job and should be punished. Similarly, a fair-minded person would not support the idea that somebody should be allowed to get away with supplying defective ladders. That, however, is not the law of tort.

In a case such as *Barnett*, the doctor is not liable in tort for the patient's death. The doctor may be punished in a disciplinary hearing for letting down the values of the profession, but he or she is not legally liable for the death of the patient –

it was the arsenic that killed the patient. In other words, the relevant cause of the harm was the drinking of the arsenic in the tea, and the doctor's negligence is regarded as remote – it is simply too far removed from the damage.

The 'but for' test is open to further criticism as it struggles to determine causation where there are successive, simultaneous or uncertain causes of harm. Its real value lies in situations where the cause of the loss or damage is easily identifiable. However, problems are caused where the facts before the court are not clear enough to show a connection between the damage caused and the conduct of the defendant.

Civil Liability Act 1961

The Civil Liability Act 1961 was passed to remedy some of the shortfalls of the factual test. The Act has established another legal action known as concurrent liability. A concurrent wrongdoer is a person who is responsible along with another or others for the damage or injury caused to the plaintiff, but it is not possible, as a matter of fact, to determine exactly who did what and who is responsible. The Act says that in these circumstances the wrongdoers are jointly liable for that damage.

A person might become a concurrent wrongdoer in a number of ways:

- *Vicarious liability.* This occurs where a person is legally responsible for the actions of another. It most often occurs in the area of employment law, where an employer is held liable for the actions of an employee. It is a very important basis of liability in the area of medical or clinical negligence as the wrongdoer is often an employee of a hospital or the HSE.
- *Breach of a joint duty.* Where two or more persons are under a joint duty of care, it is not necessary to show which of those persons breached the duty. The fact of its breach is sufficient. Again, this has particular significance in the area of medical or clinical negligence, where procedures are often lengthy and complicated and involve numerous personnel.
- *Conspiracy or concerted action.* In the case of a conspiracy or concerted action towards a common end, or alternatively where the acts are independent but cause the same damage, the same principle would apply as covered in the previous point.

The following example serves to illustrate the above scenarios. A surgeon is operating to remove the tonsils of the patient when her scalpel slips and severs the artery, causing a huge and rapid loss of blood. The theatre nurse receives such a shock at this river of blood that she injects a large amount of oxygen into the patient's vein, causing a fatal embolism. If one was to use the 'but for' test, it could be argued that both surgeon and theatre nurse would not be liable, as it would not be possible to determine who actually killed the patient. If they were employees of the hospital, however, the hospital would be vicariously liable for the actions of both. Similarly, under the second principle, they could both be held to have breached their respective duty of care towards the patient and therefore would be jointly liable. Finally, whether their actions were regarded as independent or in concert, they could be held jointly liable in terms of the third principle.

These crucial developments in the area of medical malpractice law mean that in cases where a patient cannot pinpoint the exact or relevant cause of damage amongst a number of potential causes, it will not necessarily mean that the plaintiff must lose the case.

Another approach that has found favour in the High Court is what is known as the 'material and substantial factor test' or the 'material contribution test', which is very similar to the test used by the British House of Lords (in *McGhee v National Coal Board* [1972] 3 All ER 1008, for example) and is essentially a recognition that policy needs to play a large part in determining questions of causation. Legalism must give way to pragmatism.

The High Court decision in *Superquinn Ltd v Bray Urban District Council and Others* [1998] 3 IR 542 is a good example of this approach.

Facts: The plaintiff owned a supermarket at Castle Street, Bray, County Wicklow. As a result of a violent storm, the River Dargle overflowed its banks and caused extensive damage to the goods in the supermarket. The defendant was carrying out drainage construction works in the area prior to the storm and the plaintiff alleged that the damage was caused or at least worsened by the manner in which the drainage construction works were being carried out just before the storm.

Issue before the court: Were the defendants (Bray Urban District Council and the contractors) negligent?

Decision of the court: The plaintiff's claim failed with the court finding that the defendants were not negligent. However, in its reasoning the High Court seemed to accept that a new approach to causation was necessary:

> It seems to me that . . . if it could be established that there were two causes of the damage to the plaintiff's property, the wrongdoing of the defendant and vis major, there should be an apportionment so that the defendant should only be liable for the damage attributable to its wrongdoing. The head-note in the report bears out this interpretation. Interpreted thus, the decision does not give rise to any conceptual difficulties in this post Civil Liability Act era. [. . .]
>
> Mr. Prendiville's observations, in my view, are the most reliable record we have of what happened on the night and I accept Professor Cunnane's analysis of those observations as to the significance of the breach in the flooding of the Little Bray area. In my view, it has not been demonstrated that water flowing through the breach was a material element or a significant factor in the flooding of the Plaintiff's premises. In relation to the afflux at the bridge, whatever the correct measurement of the afflux, in my view, the Plaintiff has not established that the drainage construction works, rather than natural processes, were a material element or a substantial factor in creating it.

The High Court seemed to accept that the test for causation is the material element or substantial factor test, which is often called the material contribution test. This again could be significant in the area of clinical negligence as it is clearly an expansion of the traditional 'but for' test. For example, where it can be shown that a medical practitioner's negligence significantly decreased a patient's chances of survival (as opposed to directly causing the patient's death), this would allow the court to find that the increased risk to the patient was a material contribution to the patient's death. In other words, the material contribution test, which is traditionally used in the assessment of damages, could now be used in deciding questions of causation.

This development need not mean that the plaintiff will always succeed. If the plaintiff can prove material contribution to risk/damage by the defendant, the evidentiary burden is then transferred to the defendant to disprove causation (which is very similar in practice to the *res ipsa loquitor* presumption). The plaintiff will succeed only if the defendant is thereafter unable to disprove causation.

A word of caution must be sounded: these alternative tests for causation should not be applied in every instance where the traditional 'but for' test causes a plaintiff difficulty in discharging the onus. The law must be developed cautiously and with equitable principles, rather than as a flawed product of knee-jerk decisions. However, the use of alternative formulations to the traditional test might be appropriate where there are various sources of risk and/or damage and it is difficult to determine precisely which one caused the plaintiff's injuries.

In the English decision of *Fairchild v Glenhaven Funeral Services* [2002] 3 All ER 305, the House of Lords held that causation could be established where the defendant's act 'materially increased the risk' of the injury arising. This would seem to indicate that the wider test for factual causation is now an accepted part of English law. It would be reasonable to suggest that it is only a matter of time before it is fully accepted in Ireland.

Legal causation or proximate cause

Even where the plaintiff proves factual causation, it cannot be guaranteed that he or she will win the case as the court may still find that the defendant's action or omission was not the legal cause of the injury to the plaintiff. Essentially this comes down to the court deciding, as a matter of policy, that the defendant should not be liable, despite factually causing the harm.

The most important factor in the test for legal causation is foreseeability. If the reasonable person in the shoes of the defendant could not have foreseen that his or her actions or omissions could cause the harm suffered by the plaintiff, the defendant will escape liability. Therefore, even where, as a matter of fact, the defendant has caused the plaintiff's injury, the defendant will escape liability if that injury was not foreseeable at the time of acting.

Another test used in deciding legal causation is the intervening act, the *novus actus interveniens*, where that intervening act breaks the chain of causation between the plaintiff's injury and the defendant's action by replacing the defendant's act as the sole cause of the plaintiff's harm.

A question of policy

When considering legal causation, the breadth of the factors that the court might take into consideration is too great for the scope of this book, but essentially the questions of policy are very similar to the questions that the court might ask in deciding foreseeability in the duty of care inquiry. The court, in addition to deciding on foreseeability, will consider factors such as the magnitude of the risk, the burden of taking precautions, the utility (usefulness) of the defendant's conduct, and what is common or established practice in determining the reasonableness of the defendant's conduct.

These policy factors become very important in the context of health care, where there are often budgetary and other restraints that do not make it possible for the HSE or a hospital to take every precaution. Even in instances where it can be shown that there is a factual link between the actions of the health service provider and the harm caused to a patient, the court might find as a matter of policy that the health service provider could not have reasonably prevented the harm.

The eggshell skull rule

In essence, this rule says that 'you take your plaintiffs as you find them'. If a patient has certain characteristics or a constitution that aggravates the original harm, the medical practitioner is liable for that increased damage, despite the fact that he or she could not foresee it. What is important is that the medical practitioner could foresee the original harm, which thereafter becomes worse due to the patient's make-up. It is for this reason that hospitals have extensive questionnaires for patients to complete on admission, which represent an attempt to discover any hidden characteristics.

This rule can have harsh effects, particularly in the area of psychological damage. An Irish example is the decision in *McCarthy v Murphy* [1998] IEHC 23.

Facts: As a result of the defendant's negligence, his car collided with the plaintiff's stationary car. The accident was not serious as the impact was slight. The plaintiff suffered minor whiplash. However, due to an existing psychological condition, the plaintiff developed a serious depressive reaction.

Issue before the court: If it was accepted that the defendant should have foreseen that the plaintiff might suffer whiplash as a result of the defendant's negligent driving, could the defendant be held liable for the resulting injury arising from that whiplash, namely the depressive reaction?

Decision of the court: The Supreme Court applied the thin skull or eggshell skull rule and found that the defendant was liable for the depressive reaction:

> It was argued on behalf of the Defendant that he was only liable for injury which was of a type which was reasonably foreseeable, and that

it was not foreseeable that any form of psychological injury would occur as a result of a very minor traffic accident such as in this case. The Defendant accepts the principles of the eggshell skull cases, but seeks to distinguish this case by saying that, while it could be foreseen that even a minor accident could cause physical damage such as a soft tissue injury, it was not reasonably foreseeable that that in turn would lead to a depressive condition.

I do not think I can accept that argument. [. . .]

I am of the view, on the medical evidence, that the immediate cause of the Plaintiff's depression was the soft tissue injury which she suffered in the accident. Of course the Defendant could not have anticipated that she was a person with a pre-disposition to depression, but he could have reasonably foreseen a soft tissue injury, and that being so, he is liable for damage which flows from that injury, as he has to take the Plaintiff as he finds her.

This approach has been criticised by those who argue that it is an exception to the test of foreseeability. Others argue that this approach is a variety of the test of foreseeability and is therefore justified as what must be foreseeable is the original harm, and not the extent of the harm. They argue that it is not an exception to the foreseeability rule when the extent of the harm is increased by an individual's personal characteristics because the rule has never been that you must be able to foresee the extent of the damage, but only the nature of the damage itself.

Damages and causation: summary

1   Damages are a financial award made by a court to one of the parties to an action as part of the judgment of that court. They are compensation for the harm or damages suffered by that injured party and are paid by the wrongdoer party (the tortfeasor).

2   Damages attempt to reverse the damage done by placing the injured person in either the position they were in before the harm occurred to them or the position they would have been in if the legal duty that was owed to them had in fact been performed.

3   Damages for personal injury are divided into special damages (damages capable of precise calculation) and general damages (the amount is decided at the discretion of the court). There also might be an award of aggravated damages, where the plaintiff is compensated for the effects of the defendant's conduct after the wrong was committed.

4   In medical negligence cases, the most common damages are for medical expenses and loss of wages (both special damages) and pain and suffering (general damages).

5   In order to prosecute a claim for negligence successfully, the plaintiff must demonstrate, as a matter of fact, that there is a causal connection or 'chain' between the defendant's conduct and the plaintiff's damage.

6   The factual causation test, or 'but for' test, goes along the lines of 'but for the defendant's conduct, would the plaintiff have suffered harm?' This test is very effective when the facts are clear and easy to establish, but fails where the cause of the damage cannot be adequately or accurately ascertained, usually due to the fact that science or technology is not yet sufficiently advanced to pinpoint a cause of the damage, or where there are concurrent wrongdoers. These scenarios often arise in medical negligence cases. There have been numerous attempts, particularly in medical negligence cases, to modify the 'but for' test to ease the extremely onerous burden of proof on the plaintiff where there is evidence that the defendant at least contributed to the injuries suffered by the plaintiff.

7   The courts have held that the 'but for' test is the first stage in establishing causation and in special circumstances the courts can depart from this test. These departures are often called the tests for 'legal causation' and are essentially based on public policy considerations where it would be against the interests of society to allow a factual chain of causation to incur damages.

8   The Civil Liability Act 1961 has removed a number of the obstacles previously experienced by the plaintiff seeking to prove damages, particularly where there are multiple or concurrent defendants.

Further reading

Bal, B. S. 'An introduction to medical malpractice in the USA', *Clinical Orthopaedics and Related Research* 467 (2009), 339–47.

Douglas, T. 'Medical injury compensation – beyond "no-fault"', *Medical Law* 17/30 (2009), 1–14.

Healy, J. 'A cause wrapped up in a duty', *Dublin University Law Journal* 12/1 (2005), 260a.

Murphy, E. 'No fault compensation for medical negligence', *Irish Law Times* 7 (1989), 216.

Ryan, R. and Ryan, D. '"A lost cause?" Causation in negligence cases: recent Irish developments – Part I', *Irish Law Times* 24 (2006), 91.

Ryan, R. and Ryan, D. '"A lost cause?" Causation in negligence cases: recent Irish developments – Part II', *Irish Law Times* 24 (2006), 107.

Stauch, M. '"Material contribution" as a response to causal uncertainty: time for a rethink', *Cambridge Law Journal* 68/1 (2009), 27–30.

Turton, G. 'Factual and legal causation – their relation to negligence in nursing', *British Journal of Nursing* 18 (2009), 825–7.

Useful websites

Beauchamps Solicitors ('Healthcare Update'): www.beauchamps.ie
McCann FitzGerald (solicitors): www.mccannfitzgerald.ie

chapter 8

INFORMED CONSENT TO MEDICAL TREATMENT: CAPACITY TO CONSENT

Learning outcomes

At the completion of this chapter the reader should know and understand:

- The legal concept of informed consent.
- The requirements that need to be proven by the person alleging informed consent, namely: capacity, disclosure and voluntariness.
- With regard to the concept of capacity, the use of the *Re C* test and its application by the High Court in the decision of *Fitzpatrick v FK*.
- With regard to the concept of capacity, the main provisions of the Mental Capacity Bill 2008 and the subsequent report of the Law Reform Commission.

Informed Consent

The phrase 'informed consent' means that patients must be properly informed, in language and concepts that they can understand, about the probable consequences of a treatment before consent to that treatment is sought. If the medical professional fails to obtain consent, there is a battery. If the medical professional fails to properly inform the patient about a proposed treatment to which the patient thereafter consents, there is negligence.

There are two steps in ensuring informed consent. First, there must be general consent to the touching involved in any medical treatment or even diagnosis. Second, there must be informed consent to the specific treatment that is proposed for the patient. This can happen only as a result of the medical professional properly informing the patient of the nature of the treatment and the proposed outcome, including the consequences of the treatment and the attendant risks of that treatment, in such a way that the patient properly understands the explanation.

In order for there to be a valid consent from the patient, three factors must exist:

- The patient must have the capacity to consent. This means that the patient must have sufficient mental faculties to appreciate the nature and consequences of his or her actions and the nature and consequences of the treatment in question.
- The nature and consequences of the treatment must be fully disclosed to the patient. This includes the risks usually associated with such treatment, which are often called the material risks.
- The consent must be given voluntarily by the patient.

These three essential ingredients of informed consent – capacity, disclosure and voluntariness – will be examined in detail in this and the following two chapters.

Capacity of the Patient to Give Informed Consent

A person's capacity or competency is always measured in terms of his or her ability to do a specific thing. Capacity in the legal sense can be described as the ability of a person to do something that has legal consequences.

We say that a person has the capacity to consent to medical treatment if that person can understand the need for the treatment, the consequences and risks of the treatment and what would happen if he or she refused that treatment.

Accordingly, the British Medical Association says the following in its *Consent Tool Kit* (London: BMA, 2001, p.8):

> To demonstrate capacity individuals should be able to:
> - understand in simple language what the medical treatment is, its purpose and nature, and why it is being proposed;
> - understand its principal benefits, risks and alternatives;
> - understand in broad terms what will be the consequences of not receiving the proposed treatment;
> - retain the information for long enough to make an effective decision; and
> - make a free choice (i.e. free from pressure).

This approach to capacity is often referred to as the functional approach because it considers whether the patient is able, at the time when a particular decision has to be made, to understand the nature and effects of that particular decision, focusing on the functioning of the individual with regard to understanding and appreciating the issues involved in that decision. In short, the functional approach to assessing capacity is time-specific and issue-specific.

The fact that a person has the capacity to perform one type of legal act does not automatically mean that he or she has the capacity to perform all sorts of other legal acts. A person's capacity must be measured at the time in relation to that specific act. The converse is also true: the fact that a person is found to be incapacitated to do a certain legal act does not disqualify him or her from doing any other legal acts. Each situation is regarded separately.

It would be a cumbersome process, however, to assess somebody's capacity every time he or she is called upon to make a decision and therefore a person is deemed (which means that the law will take it as a fact until the contrary is proved) to have the capacity to give true consent when that person is an adult (over the age of eighteen years) and possessed of a sound mind. When something is 'deemed' it means that presumptions are created – so a person over the age of eighteen is presumed to be capable of consent until the evidence clearly shows that he or she lacks capacity.

Similarly, a patient may have the capacity to make some but not all treatment decisions. This will depend on the complexity of the treatment or procedure and the complexity of the explanation by the health professional concerning, for example, the benefits, consequences and side effects of such a treatment or procedure. For example, a sixteen-year-old child can consent to having a cut stitched but may not be sufficiently intellectually developed to consent properly to heart surgery or chemotherapy. In other words, a patient's capacity must be assessed in light of the decision the patient is being asked to make. For this reason the phrase 'relative capacity' is often used, because the capacity is measured in relation to the task that the patient is required to perform, which is pretty much the same as the functional approach.

The situation of a mentally incapacitated adult presents two immediate problems in Irish law. First, how is one to decide whether a patient is mentally incapacitated? Second, if mental incapacity is established, who is authorised to consent on that patient's behalf?

The law is not fixated on the symptoms or manifestations of a patient's mental illness or disability, but rather whether the person can understand the nature and consequences of the proposed treatment and, in the light of that understanding, make a decision whether to have that treatment or not. The fact that a patient suffers from some mental disability must be taken into account, but does not automatically disqualify the patient from giving consent or from refusing treatment. Where it is clear that the patient fully understands the nature and consequences of the proposed treatment, the health professional would be acting reasonably in accepting the consent of the patient. Of course, the health professional should be absolutely certain in his or her mind that the patient is giving informed consent, knowing the background of the patient.

This is really about human rights such as the right to autonomy, the right to self-determination and the right to dignity. Simply labelling somebody as 'mentally ill' or 'intellectually disabled' and thereafter ignoring their wishes would strip that person of even the most basic human rights.

Re C (an adult) (refusal of medical treatment) FD [1994] 1 All ER 819 was an important English decision, which has subsequently provided valuable guidelines in determining the capacity of a person who has been medically diagnosed as mentally ill or intellectually disabled.

Facts: A patient diagnosed as a paranoid schizophrenic, and who was detained in Broadmoor special hospital for mentally disordered offenders, was advised to have an amputation below the knee of a grossly infected (gangrenous) lower leg. The patient refused the amputation and the hospital sought the guidance of the court as to whether the patient's schizophrenia affected his capacity to consent to, or in this case refuse, medical treatment.

Issue before the court: Did the patient have the necessary capacity to make the decision to keep his leg, even if this might result in his death, and bearing in mind that he was a diagnosed paranoid schizophrenic who periodically displayed psychotic symptoms?

Decision of the court: The court stated that three questions needed to be asked in determining the mental capacity of a patient to consent to, or refuse, treatment. Could the patient comprehend and retain the necessary information? Was the patient able to believe it? Was the patient able to weigh the information, balancing risks and needs, so as to arrive at a choice?

These questions need to be more closely examined. First, is the patient able to comprehend and retain the necessary information? In other words, did the mental illness complained of prevent the patient from storing information in order to mull over that information before making a decision. As certain mental illnesses, for example Alzheimer's disease, attack the memory directly, the nature of the disease and its direct impact on the memory need to be carefully considered.

Is the patient able to believe the information given to him or her? If the patient cannot take the health professional seriously or thinks that the health professional is part of a greater conspiracy against the patient, then clearly the patient will not believe the information being given by that health professional. The fact that a person is a diagnosed paranoid schizophrenic is clearly important when considering this second requirement. Again, the prudent health professional will not merely rely on the diagnosis, but will rather question the patient on why the medical advice is being refused. If the patient replies that the doctor is 'one of them' or words to that effect, then the health professional has grounds to believe that the patient fails on this second leg of the capacity test.

Is the patient able to consider and weigh the information, including balancing the risks against the advantages and needs, and finally arrive at a decision? The final test involves an assessment of the patient's cognitive abilities to understand and assess the medical advice, including both 'pros' and 'cons', and thereafter to make a considered decision. In other words, the brain power and relative intelligence of the patient will need to be assessed in relation to the nature and complexity of the medical advice presented. A person with a learning disability may succeed on the first two legs of the test, but not be able to assess or analyse the information sufficiently to make an informed decision, and so could fail on the last leg.

In *Re C*, the court held that despite being diagnosed as a paranoid schizophrenic, the patient did have the necessary mental capacity to refuse to give consent to the amputation.

Medical professionals need to question patients closely to ensure that their decisions, whether consent or refusal, are made in accordance with the three questions laid down in *Re C*. Assessment of capacity is not deciding whether a rational person would make the same or a similar decision, as it is not the decision that is ultimately examined but the thought process in reaching that decision. And where there is a medical disorder, it is not the particular diagnosis that implies incapacity but the patient's specific disabilities and their impact on his or her thought process at the time that the patient is required to decide.

Of course, it is usually only in situations of refusal that a patient's capacity is challenged and closely examined, and one must wonder whether there is always true consent where a patient with an intellectual disability or mental illness agrees to treatment that has been recommended by the professional.

Who decides for the incapacitated patient?

There is a widespread misconception that the patient's family must always be consulted and the ultimate decision left to them with regard to a patient who does not have the capacity to decide whether to accept medical treatment. This is not true and it would breach the principles of confidentiality and autonomy.

An adult person is not entitled, by reason only of blood or marriage, to consent on behalf of another adult. In order to consent on behalf of another adult, the person seeking to supply the consent must be authorised by law to supply that consent. The fact that one is a relative by marriage or a member of the family does not, by itself, confer any authority on a person to consent on behalf of another person.

Where the doctor or nurse needs to treat a patient who does not have the capacity to consent to treatment, there are two alternatives. First, there could be a reliance on the defence of necessity if the situation was, or became, an emergency where the incapacitated patient needed to be treated in order to avoid death or permanent and serious damage.

The second alternative is an application to make the incapacitated patient a ward of court, which will establish the President of the High Court or of the Circuit Court as the patient's guardian, able to make choices on his or her behalf (usually on the advice of a wardship committee). The court will always regard the patient's best interests as the most important consideration when making decisions about his or her treatment. This is often problematic as it is not always clear what the best interests of the patient are and there may be differing opinions as to what is best for the patient and whether the proposed treatment is in the best interests of the patient. This procedure is complicated and expensive. From a financial point of view, it is generally justified only when there are substantial assets involved.

Accordingly, most people who cannot make decisions for themselves are in a sort of legal limbo as they do not have legally recognised representatives acting on their behalf. It is for this reason that it is such a common practice for health professionals to seek consent from family members concerning proposed medical treatment. From a strict legal point of view, these family members have no right to consent on behalf of the patient, but from a practical point of view, the health professional has no other option.

The leading Irish case dealing with issues of consenting to treatment, or in this case to the withdrawal of treatment, on behalf of an intellectually disabled patient is *Re a Ward of Court* [1995] 2 ILRM 401. In this case the Supreme Court authorised the removal of a feeding tube from a patient in a near persistent vegetative state (PVS) after her family had sought permission to do this. The majority of the Supreme Court held that the right to life guaranteed by the Constitution necessarily implied that a person had the right to die a natural and dignified death, which would include the right to refuse to have a life artificially prolonged. The rights of privacy and bodily dignity allow a patient to refuse medical treatment, even where that medical treatment might be the difference between life and death.

As the patient was not competent to decide to refuse medical treatment, the question was whether the court was entitled to make that decision for her. The Supreme Court decided that it was entitled to make that decision by virtue of the *parens patriae* power (essentially a paternalistic power), which was originally held by the Lord Chancellor of Ireland over people without legal capacity and had since been transferred to the High Court by statute.

Although this decision involved the withdrawal of treatment rather than the provision of treatment, the principles surrounding the question of capacity and ability to consent on behalf of another are essentially the same.

Capacity to Refuse Medical Treatment

A health professional is trained to save life. A patient might view death as being preferable to what he or she perceives to be an 'inferior life', particularly in circumstances where the patient excelled in his or her former lifestyle. A patient is entitled to refuse medical treatment, for whatever reason he or she chooses, as long as that patient has the capacity to make an informed decision. Only in situations where there is clear evidence that the patient lacks the mental capacity to make that decision can the medical professional approach the court to override that patient's refusal of treatment, in the best interests of the patient.

The fact that the treatment might be the best thing, in the objective sense, for that patient is not a defence to an action for battery if the patient has sufficient capacity to refuse medical treatment. The Supreme Court, in *Re a Ward of Court* [1995], recognised that a patient has the right to refuse medical treatment, even where this refusal would lead to that patient's death. However, that case involved making a decision on behalf of a patient in a persistent vegetative state. What about the patient who is conscious?

The question of the capacity of a conscious patient to refuse medical treatment was considered by the High Court in *Fitzpatrick v FK* [2008] IEHC 104.

Facts: FK was a Congolese national with limited English. She went into labour soon after arriving at hospital in the early evening and delivered the following morning. She suffered a massive haemorrhage immediately after delivery and lost well over half of her blood. She refused a blood transfusion, explaining through her friend and interpreter that she was a Jehovah's Witness and could not have a transfusion. The hospital secured a care plan outlining alternative treatments not involving blood products. The patient was treated with these authorised products and a vaginal pack was put in place in an effort to stem the bleeding.

As her condition was deteriorating, it was explained to the patient that she might die if she was not given blood. The patient responded by asking for 'Coca Cola, tomatoes and eggs'. The hospital authorities were concerned that the patient did not understand the seriousness of her situation and they applied to the High

Court (Abbot J) stating that, despite the patient being a competent adult, they were concerned about her capacity to refuse a blood transfusion.

The High Court granted the order allowing the hospital to give the patient a blood transfusion, on the grounds that the welfare of the patient's newborn child was paramount and that as the wishes of the mother might result in her own death, which would orphan the newborn child, the mother's refusal to have a blood transfusion was overruled. The patient received the blood transfusion and survived.

Issue before the court: The questions before the High Court hearing were whether the patient's constitutional right of bodily integrity had been violated and whether she was entitled to damages for trespass to the person.

Decision of the court: Laffoy J held that the hospital and the attending staff had acted lawfully in sedating the patient and administering a blood transfusion. The decision set out important principles to be followed in determining the capacity of a patient to refuse medical treatment:

- Where a patient chose to die rather than receive treatment, the doctor had to decide whether the patient had the capacity at the time to make such a momentous decision.
- The test for capacity was that outlined in *Re C*.
- If a patient assimilated and believed the information given to him or her about proposed treatment but thereafter rejected the treatment on religious grounds, then that patient had the capacity to do so in terms of *Re C* and had the right to make such refusal as an exercise of the right to religious beliefs (Article 44 of the Constitution).
- Where a patient chose to give up his or her constitutional right to life, the court would need clear and compelling proof that the patient could fully comprehend and appreciate the seriousness of the situation and the gravity of this decision.

On the evidence before it, the court held that for FK to have the necessary capacity she would have had to assimilate and believe that a blood transfusion was necessary and that she might die without it. The hospital staff members were justified in doubting that she did have the requisite capacity as she had undergone a long labour, a difficult delivery and a massive haemorrhage; in addition, there were communication difficulties because of the language differences between staff and the patient. The hospital was justified in concluding that FK did not meet the requirements of the *Re C* test and the hospital had acted lawfully in sedating FK and administering the blood transfusion.

Although the *Re C* test for capacity to refuse treatment had become established in Ireland, it was still an English decision and therefore of persuasive authority only. This 2008 Irish decision has affirmed the principles established in the *Re C* decision, which constitutes direct and binding authority.

Mental Capacity Bill 2008

On 15 September 2008 the government approved proposals for a Mental Capacity Bill. This Bill seeks to replace the wards of court system, which is the system that currently applies to people who are incapable of managing their affairs. The Bill introduces a framework that governs decision making on behalf of persons who lack capacity.

The proposed Bill sets out a number of guiding principles:

- It will be presumed, until proven otherwise, that a person has capacity. This is a restatement of the common law and ensures continuity between the existing law on this question and any future decisions.
- No intervention is to take place unless it is necessary, having regard to the needs and individual circumstances of the person, including whether the person is likely to increase or regain capacity. This might be interpreted as confirming the defence of necessity.
- A person will not be considered as unable to make a decision unless all practicable steps to help him or her make a decision have been taken without success. From an evidential point of view, this means that a person seeking to make a decision on behalf of a patient would need to show what steps have been taken to involve that person in the decision-making process, and convince the court that there are no further practicable steps that can be taken.
- A person is not to be treated as unable to make a decision merely because he or she makes an unwise decision. Again, this is a restatement of the common law. The question is not whether the person has made a decision with which the average person would agree, but whether that person understands the nature and consequences of that decision.
- Any act done or decision made under the Bill must be done or made in the way that is least restrictive of the person's rights and freedom of action. This is in keeping with the principle of proportionality, which has assumed a central role in European Union law.
- Due regard must be given to the need to respect the right of a person to dignity, bodily integrity, privacy and autonomy.
- Account must be taken of a person's past and present wishes, where ascertainable. This might open the door a little further with regard to advance directives.
- Account must be taken of the views of any person with an interest in the welfare of a person who lacks capacity, where these views have been made known. The Bill does not specify that any one person's view should be given priority over another's and therefore it would seem that all the views of all interested persons must be taken into account. This means, literally in any event, that a medical professional would need to consider the views of all interested persons when considering whether to treat and the nature of the treatment. As this would have obvious practical problems, the courts may

interpret the phrase 'any person with an interest in the welfare of a person' very restrictively. In addition, it must always be remembered that the medical professional's overriding duty is still to act in the patient's best interests, as the Bill is clear that any act or decision made under it must be done or made in the best interests of the person who lacks capacity.

The Bill establishes a presumption of capacity, which it defines as 'the ability to understand the nature and consequences of a decision in the context of available choices at the time the decision is to be made'. It states:

> . . . a person lacks the capacity to make a decision if he or she is unable–
> (a)   to understand the information relevant to the decision,
> (b)   to retain that information,
> (c)   to use or weigh that information as part of the process of making the decision, or
> (d)   to communicate his or her decision . . .

As these questions will be decided by a civil court, the standard of proof is that of a balance of probabilities, which means that the court will need to weigh which version is the most probable, whether that person has capacity or whether that person does not have capacity.

An interesting principle recognised by the Bill is the entitlement to supported decision making. The person must, so far as is reasonably practicable, be permitted to participate, or to improve his or her ability to participate, as fully as possible in any act done for him or her and in any decision affecting him or her. Where it is not possible to support a person in this way, the court or a court-appointed personal guardian will act as the substitute decision maker.

Before a medical practitioner performs any act in connection with the personal care, health care or treatment of another person whose decision-making capacity is in doubt, he or she must comply with the following requirements:

- Before doing the act, take reasonable steps to establish whether the person lacks capacity in relation to the matter in question.
- When doing the act, reasonably believe that the other person lacks capacity in relation to the matter in question and it is in the other person's best interests that the act be done.

If the medical professional follows these steps, the Bill grants him or her immunity from liability for, one must assume, actions in battery.

Where the Circuit Court or High Court finds that a person does lack capacity, it can appoint a personal guardian to that person. This guardian is empowered to make decisions concerning the incapacitated individual's personal welfare or property and affairs. However, decisions on certain matters of grave proportions such as non-therapeutic sterilisation, withdrawal of artificial life-sustaining treatment or organ donation will be made only in the High Court.

These persons appointed by the court to act on behalf of incapacitated persons will be supervised by the Office of Public Guardian, which is a body that will be created when the Bill becomes an Act. The office can also step in and act as a guardian when there is nobody to act as a guardian for a specific person.

The concept of capacity used in the Bill

At first the definition of capacity in the Bill, for all intents and purposes, seems to be a formulation of the *Re C* test. However, it is important to realise that before one can use the *Re C* test the appropriate context must be established to justify its use. It cannot arbitrarily be used in any context. In other words, before the *Re C* test can be used, there should exist objective factors that seriously challenge the presumption of capacity. For example, in the *Re C* case itself, the patient under consideration was a diagnosed paranoid schizophrenic, and in *Fitzpatrick v FK*, the patient under consideration had immediately prior to her decision gone through a long labour, a difficult birth and a massive blood loss, not to mention the practical difficulties of language and comprehension.

What becomes apparent concerning the definition of capacity in the Bill is that there is no defined 'prerequisite context' justifying its application. For example, in the Mental Health Act 2001, for the Act to be applicable in the first place, there must be a finding that the person under consideration for involuntary admission is suffering from a 'mental disorder', which in turn is defined as constituting either a 'mental illness', 'severe dementia' or a 'significant intellectual disability', and again these conditions are in turn defined. In other words, in the current definition found in the Bill, there needs to be a diagnostic step as a prerequisite to the use of the capacity definition. In addition, it needs to be clearly spelt out who is entitled to make this diagnostic step.

Another aspect of the Bill of particular concern to medical professionals is that its focus seems to be on long-term incapacity, rather than interim or short-term incapacity. Whilst there is provision for interim orders, which can be obtained from the court on the grounds of urgency, there does not seem to be a provision covering the situation where there is no time to go to court and a decision about treatment needs to be made and implemented immediately. The existing practice would be to ask permission from the person's next of kin. Although this is not strictly legal, it is an inevitable consequence of the high costs and lengthy delays currently associated with ward of court applications. A solution would seem to be to make provision, in emergency situations, that the medical professional could seek the consent of the next of kin to carry out emergency treatment. A decision-making hierarchy would need to be specified in the event of differing opinions amongst the next of kin. This would clothe the existing practice with legality and would also ensure minimum disruption of this current practice.

Personal guardians will be appointed by the court and will be given the same powers as donees under an enduring power of attorney. Their powers will include 'giving or refusing consent to the carrying out or continuation of a treatment by a person providing health care for the person who lacks capacity'. Section 10 of the Bill states: 'A personal guardian appointed by the court shall be an individual who has reached 18 years of age and is otherwise deemed suitable by the court to be so appointed.'

These personal guardians do not need to hold any qualifications or practice experience and therefore the Bill contemplates the delegation of this decision-making power to anyone who acts in good faith and in accordance with the basic principles set out in the beginning of the Bill. In practice, this could mean that lay carers and others without any formal qualification at all may be in a position to take decisions on behalf of a service user with limited or no capacity. Whilst this may make sense from the point of view of resources, it does introduce the prospect of inappropriate action, whether intentional or misguided, on behalf of people who cannot protect themselves against exploitation and abuse.

Section 11 of the Bill places restrictions on the powers of an appointed personal guardian. A personal guardian may not:

- Make decisions on behalf of a person if that person has capacity to make his or her own decision about that particular matter and that personal guardian knows or should reasonably know this.
- Stop a named person from having contact with the person lacking capacity.
- Arbitrarily replace a person responsible for the health care of the person lacking capacity with another.
- Deal with the property of the person lacking capacity.
- Make a decision inconsistent with a decision made by a donee under an enduring power of attorney.
- Order life-sustaining treatment to be stopped in respect of the person lacking capacity.
- Restrain (including using or threatening to use force to make the person do something or to restrict the person's liberty or movement) the person lacking capacity unless that authority has been expressly conferred by the court; the person lacking capacity lacks it in relation to the issue in question; or it is necessary to prevent harm to the person lacking capacity and the restraint is a proportionate response to the likelihood of the person suffering harm or the seriousness of that harm.

The power to make decisions on behalf of incapacitated persons is not restricted to the court-appointed personal guardian. Section 16 of the Bill also provides for 'informal decision making'. The Bill provides that a person may do an act 'in connection with the personal care, health care or treatment of another person whose decision-making capacity is in doubt' provided that 'it is in the other person's best interests that the act be done' and the person:

- Takes reasonable steps before doing that act to establish whether the other person lacks capacity in relation to the matter in question.
- Reasonably believes that the other person lacks capacity in relation to the matter in question.

The person will not be liable for any wrongdoing if his or her action would have been lawful had the other person had the capacity to consent to that action and had consented to that action.

The Bill goes on to suggest that the person can take money from the other person in compensation for any expense incurred in carrying out the action. The person can still be liable for negligence or criminal acts in carrying out the action.

Section 20 makes it clear that the Bill has not changed the law regarding capacity and consent in specific contexts, namely:

(a) capacity and consent to marriage or civil partnership
(b) consent to a judicial separation, a divorce or a dissolution of a civil partnership
(c) consent to a child being placed for adoption
(d) consent to the making of an adoption order
(e) consent to have sexual relations
(f) voting at an election or at a referendum
(g) acting as a member of a jury.

Similarly, Section 21 makes it clear that certain matters can only be dealt with by the High Court (and not by a Circuit Court and definitely not by a personal guardian) concerning a person who lacks decision-making capacity. Such matters are in connection with non-therapeutic sterilisation, withdrawal of artificial life-sustaining treatment, and organ donation.

Section 27 says that where a person, be it a donee or a personal guardian (or, presumably, an informal decision maker), has the care of another person who lacks capacity and ill-treats or wilfully neglects the person lacking capacity, he or she is guilty of an offence. If that person is thereafter charged and summarily convicted (a trial without jury), he or she may receive a term of imprisonment up to twelve months and/or a fine up to €3,000. If that person is convicted on indictment (trial by jury), he or she may be imprisoned for up to five years and/or receive a fine up to €50,000.

Unfortunately, the Bill does not contain an interpretation section. It would be helpful to have a full definition of 'health care'. The only clue is that there is a distinction between 'health care' and 'life-sustaining treatment' in the 'Enduring Powers of Attorney' chapter and therefore whilst various forms of medical treatment might be included under both heads, clearly other forms of health care will not.

Advance Care Directives

On the subject of the enduring power of attorney (sometimes known as 'the living will') it is interesting to note that there was a Private Member's Bill (a proposal from the opposition in the Oireachtas) entitled 'Advance Healthcare Decisions Bill 2010'. It is unlikely to be enacted but it will increase the pressure on the government to introduce much-needed legislation in this area. It adds to a Law Reform Commission report entitled *Bioethics: Advance Care Directives*, published on 16 September 2009, which recommends that legislation be introduced and includes a draft Mental Capacity (Advance Care Directives) Bill.

The Commission made the following recommendations with regard to advance care directives:

- The proposed legislation should be facilitative in nature and be seen in the wider context of a process of health care planning by an individual, whether in a general health care setting or in the context of hospice care;
- The proposed legislation would not alter or affect the existing criminal law under which euthanasia and assisted suicide is prohibited;
- The proposed legislation would apply to advance care directives by adults involving refusal of treatment, for example: 'I do not wish to receive a flu injection' or 'I do not wish to be resuscitated';
- A person could refuse treatment on religious grounds;
- An advance care directive could, in general, be verbal or written;
- Under the proposed legislation, an advance care directive could include an instruction to refuse life-sustaining treatment (treatment which is intended to sustain or prolong life and that replaces or maintains the operation of vital bodily functions that are incapable of independent operation); this type would have to be in writing and witnessed;
- The proposed legislation would allow for the nomination of a health care proxy to carry out the person's wishes;
- The Commission recommends that a person could not refuse basic care, (such as warmth, shelter, palliative care, oral nutrition and hydration and hygiene measures);
- The Commission recommends that a statutory Code of Practice on Advance Care Directives should contain detailed guidance for health care professionals, including the circumstances in which artificial nutrition and hydration (ANH) may be considered to be basic care or, as the case may be, artificial life-sustaining treatment;
- The Commission recommends that a person should be encouraged to seek medical advice when making an advance care directive, but it would not be mandatory;
- A health care professional would not have any legal liability where

they follow an advance care directive that they believe to be valid and to be applicable to the condition being treated;

- The proposed legislation would not prohibit a professional body from investigating whether the failure to carry out an advance care directive was in breach of professional standards; if that happened, a health care professional would have a full defence if they acted in good faith;

- The Commission also recommends that the proposed legislation on advance care directives should be incorporated into the Government's proposed overhaul of the law on mental capacity, contained in the Scheme of a Mental Capacity Bill 2008.

Capacity to give informed consent: summary

1   Consent to treatment must always be obtained from a patient; treatment without consent is battery.

2   For there to be a genuine consent to medical treatment, the patient must have the capacity to consent; the nature, benefits and risks of the proposed treatment must be disclosed and explained to the patient; and the patient must be allowed to make a choice without any pressure or coercion from the health professional.

3   Capacity is the ability to do something. In legal terms, capacity is a relative concept as a person's legal capacity is measured in relation to a specific task to be performed at a specific time.

4   The capacity to consent to medical treatment includes the capacity to refuse treatment. A health professional must respect the wishes of a patient as long as that patient has the capacity to accept or refuse medical treatment.

5   An adult person is presumed to have capacity until the contrary is proved.

6   A patient suffering from an intellectual disability may still have capacity to consent to medical treatment, depending on the nature and extent of that disability and the complexity of the proposed treatment.

7   A health professional must ascertain the capacity of a patient to consent to, or refuse, medical treatment by determining whether the patient has the cognitive abilities to remember and therefore consider the medical treatment in question, whether the patient believes the description and advice given by that health professional, and whether the patient has the intellectual capacity to balance the benefits against the risks of the proposed treatment.

8   The presence or absence of the capacity to consent is a question of fact that is decided on legal principles rather than medical principles. Although the court will be assisted in arriving at its decision by medical professionals, the decision is for the court alone to make.

9   The Mental Capacity Bill 2008 seeks to implement a number of radical departures from the common law with respect to the question of capacity and the right of another person to act on behalf of an incapacitated patient.

10   The concept of the advance care directive (often called a living will) is the subject of a Law Reform Commission report entitled *Bioethics: Advance Care Directives*, which contains many far-reaching recommendations with regard to proposed legislation.

Further reading

Cornock, M. and Jones, H. 'Consent and the child in action: a legal commentary', *Paediatric Nursing* 22 (2010), 14–20.

Daly, B. 'Patient consent, the anaesthetic nurse and the peri-operative environment: Irish law and informed consent', *British Journal of Anaesthetic & Recovery Nursing* 10/1 (2009), 3–10.

Dimond, B. 'Mental capacity and decision making: defining capacity', *British Journal of Nursing* 16 (2007), 1138–9.

Dolgin, J. L. 'The legal development of the informed consent doctrine: past and present', *Cambridge Quarterly of Healthcare Ethics* 19 (2010), 97–109.

Donnelly, M. 'The right of autonomy in Irish law', *Medico-Legal Journal of Ireland* 14 (2008), 34–40.

Goldworth, A. 'A suggested change in the informed consent procedure', *Cambridge Quarterly of Healthcare Ethics* 19 (2010), 258–60.

Gunn, M. J., Wong, J. G., Clare, I. C. H. and Holland, A. J. 'Decision-making capacity', *Medical Law Review* 7 (1999), 269–306.

Habiba, M. A. 'Examining consent within the patient–doctor relationship', *Journal of Medical Ethics* 26 (2000), 183–7.

Hendriks, A. 'Personal autonomy, good care, informed consent and human dignity – some reflections from a European perspective', *Medicine and Law* 28 (2009), 469.

Kapp, M. P. H. 'Legal issues arising in the process of determining decisional capacity in older persons', *Care Management Journals* 11 (2010), 101–7.

Keys, M. 'Capacity – whose decision is it anyway?' paper delivered at the Law and Mental Health Conference, Law Faculty, NUI Galway, 17 November 2007.

McMahon, S. 'A patient advocate's perspective: consent', *Medico-Legal Journal of Ireland* 14 (2008), 62–5.

O'Keeffe, S. 'A clinician's perspective: issues of capacity in care', *Medico-Legal Journal of Ireland* 14 (2008), 41–50.

Raymundo, M. M. and Goldim, J. R. 'Moral-psychological development related to the capacity of adolescents and elderly patients to consent', *Journal of Medical Ethics* 34 (2008), 602–5.

Rikkert, M. G., van den Bercken, J. H., ten Have, H. A. and Hoefnagels, W. H. 'Experienced consent in geriatrics research: a new method to optimize the capacity to consent in frail elderly subjects', *Journal of Medical Ethics* 23 (1997), 271–6.

Van Staden, C. W. and Krüger, C. 'Incapacity to give informed consent owing to mental disorder', *Journal of Medical Ethics* 29 (2003), 41–3.

Wicclair, M. R. 'Medical paternalism in "House M.D.", *Journal of Medical Humanities* 34 (2008), 93–9.

Wicks, E. 'The right to refuse medical treatment under the European Convention on Human Rights', *Medical Law Review* 9 (2001), 17–40.

Useful websites

Irishhealth.com: www.irishhealth.com

Mental Health Ireland: www.mentalhealthireland.ie

National Disability Authority: www.nda.ie

British Medical Journal: www.bmj.com

The Lancet: www.thelancet.com

eMedicine: http://emedicine.medscape.com

American Medical Association: www.ama.assn.org

Royal College of Nursing: www.rcn.org.uk

Nursing Times: www.nursingtimes.net

Nursing & Midwifery Council (UK): www.nmc-uk.org

Boston College, School of Nursing: www.bc.edu/bc_org/avp/son/ethics

chapter 9

DISCLOSURE: WHAT THE PATIENT NEEDS TO KNOW

> *Learning outcomes*
> At the completion of this chapter the reader should know and understand:
> - The second requirement for informed consent, namely full and proper disclosure.
> - The concept of material risk.
> - The debate between proponents of the doctor-oriented approach and those of the patient-oriented approach.
> - The unique approach of the Irish courts to the question of disclosure and the difficulties that this poses for the Irish health professional.
> - The real benefits of disclosure.
> - The flawed concept of therapeutic privilege.

Full and Proper Disclosure of Material Risks

The law about disclosure can be stated in a straightforward manner: the nature and the consequences of the proposed treatment must be fully disclosed to the patient as the patient cannot consent to a procedure or treatment that he or she does not properly understand. Unfortunately, this is a lot more complicated than it at first seems.

The most obvious difficulty is who decides what is important and needs to be disclosed: the doctor or the patient? If the patient is to decide, how is the doctor to know what the patient regards as important? If the doctor is to decide, does this not mean that the doctor can withhold information that the patient might regard as crucial?

Another problem concerns what is meant by 'understanding' on the part of the patient. Doctors and nurses receive extensive training in areas such as biology, physiology and the related sciences so that they can understand the complicated functions of the human body. If a patient has not received this training, can that patient properly understand the illness or injury and the proposed treatment?

A third problem involves what is known as 'the inquisitive patient'. This is the patient who is genuinely interested in the proposed treatment and asks a lot of questions about some quite technical and complex issues, often as a result of doing some reading and research before coming into hospital. How far does the health professional need to go in answering these questions?

The question of disclosure also raises a number of legal dilemmas, which the courts in different countries answer in different ways. Perhaps the predominant cause of these legal problems is that the test of negligence, rather than the test of trespass, is applied to the issue of disclosure and the negligence test is the 'reasonable health professional' test, which means that, traditionally, members of the profession would decide whether the disclosure was sufficient or not. This does not sit well with the notion of patient autonomy, as it is the patient, and not the doctor, who should ultimately decide whether to proceed with the treatment that the doctor is proposing. Clearly a rather unique form of negligence test is needed when considering issues of disclosure, but that is a lot more difficult than it sounds.

Perhaps the most well-known case on this subject is the American case of *Canterbury v Spence* (1972) 464 F 2d 772, where the patient and his mother were not warned about the danger of paralysis from spinal surgery as the surgeon considered the chance of paralysis to be about one per cent and argued that all this warning would have done was frighten the patient away from undergoing necessary surgery. The court rejected the notion that the surgeon should decide how much to tell the patient based on professional custom and practice. It held that the court would decide how much should have been disclosed to the patient to allow the patient to make an informed decision; in other words, it was a legal question and not a medical one. The court held that a doctor should disclose all material risks that would influence the decision of a reasonable patient. Material risks means risks to which a reasonable patient would attach significance.

While this case must be applauded as an important step forward in patients' rights, it has been argued that the outcome places doctors in a difficult position by expecting them to know what a reasonable patient would consider a significant risk. Nevertheless, this can usually be determined on the basis of common sense and the gap between the reasonable doctor and the reasonable patient is not as wide as some think.

It has also been argued that many patients would rather not be told anything as what they do not know cannot scare them – an 'ignorance is bliss' approach. This might sometimes be true, but it places the doctor in a vulnerable position if the patient later complains that he or she was told nothing at all. The doctor would be well advised to insist, gently but firmly, on explaining the nature and aims of the treatment and discussing the probable outcomes (including the material risks) in a calm and sensible manner. Unless the patient sits with hands over ears and head between the knees, he or she will soon be drawn into the conversation.

A nurse has an important role to play in this area as he or she will probably know the patient better than the doctor and will be an important emotional support to the patient, encouraging the patient to participate in, rather than avoid, this crucial conversation. In addition, the nurse may know the patient well enough to determine whether he or she did in fact understand the explanation offered by the doctor, and may assist the process by asking relevant questions or determining through conversation with the patient what questions the patient wanted to ask but did not ask for some reason.

Finally, as the judgment of *Healy v HSE* shows, the nurse also has the expertise, and therefore a duty of care, to act independently on information, such as symptoms, and to keep the patient well aware of his or her situation and the possible treatment paths to pursue.

The Irish Position: Elective and Non-Elective (Therapeutic) Treatment

In *Walsh v Family Planning Services Ltd* [1992] 1 IR 496, Finlay CJ laid down a rather direct formula, namely that to 'supply the patient with the material facts is so obviously necessary to an informed choice on the part of the patient that no reasonably prudent doctor would fail to make it'.

Facts: The patient had a vasectomy operation. This was categorised by the court as an elective procedure as it was not performed to save life or avoid permanent and serious injury, but was rather for prophylactic purposes. The patient thereafter suffered from extreme pain in the testicles caused by 'an exceptionally rare and not properly accounted for consequence of vasectomy operations' called orchialgia.

Issue before the court: Should the surgeon have warned the patient about the danger of orchialgia, seeing as this is a very rare consequence of a vasectomy?

Decision of the court: The Supreme Court held that there was an obligation on the doctor to inform the patient of this condition, even if it is rare:

> On the evidence and in the circumstances of the case there was an obligation on the defendants to warn the plaintiff of the possible consequences of any condition such as orchialgia notwithstanding the rarity of its incidence, particularly since the operation was elective, rather than under any compulsion.

On the evidence, the Supreme Court was satisfied that the doctor had in fact warned the patient about the danger of suffering testicular pain after the procedure, although she had pointed out that its incidence was extremely rare. Accordingly, the doctor had made a full and proper disclosure.

The Supreme Court adopted a rather unique approach by distinguishing between elective and non-elective procedures. It held that where the procedure was non-elective (in other words, necessary to avoid permanent damage or death), the duty to inform might not be as extensive as when the procedure was elective. The supposed logic of this distinction is that in cases where the treatment is necessary to avoid death or permanent serious injury, the patient does not really have much choice but to agree to the treatment, and in those cases disclosure might not make a difference. On the other hand, where the patient chooses to undergo treatment that is not necessary to save life or limb, the patient should be fully informed before finally going ahead with the treatment or procedure.

The procedure in question, a vasectomy, was an elective procedure, as the patient would have been perfectly healthy without the procedure. Therefore, there was a more onerous duty on the surgeon or doctor to explain and discuss the risks and complications normally associated with a vasectomy. On the facts, the court was satisfied that the surgeon had done so.

The obvious problem with this distinction between elective and non-elective procedures is that it is not always as clear as the Supreme Court would have us believe. What if the patient had wanted a vasectomy because he already had two children suffering from severe intellectual disability that seemed to be genetic and he did not want any more children? What if the patient's partner could not risk another pregnancy because of severe complications in her previous pregnancy? Should a vasectomy in those contexts be regarded as elective?

The practical answer to this problem is that the doctor and nurse, when dealing with the patient, must fully explore the reasons why the patient is requesting the treatment or procedure and, if in any doubt, should choose to disclose risks rather than conceal them. The nurse, as the person who has more frequent contact with the patient, is in an ideal position to explore properly the reasons for a patient choosing to undergo a specific treatment or procedure and could thereafter fully brief the doctor or surgeon about the reasons given by the patient.

The other difficulty with this decision is that whilst Finlay CJ appeared to be adopting the established approach to questions of disclosure (as set out in *Dunne v The National Maternity Hospital* [1989] IR 91), Flaherty J seemed to be using what is known as the 'materiality test', to elective procedures at least. The other judges seemed to be choosing a bit of both. The end result was that it was not really clear which had ascendancy in Irish law: the reasonable doctor test or the reasonable patient test or the English test (as set out in *Sidaway v Board of Governors of Bethlehem Royal Hospital* [1985] AC 871), which is essentially a compromise test where the judge can override medical opinion when it is glaringly obvious that the patient would have wanted to know about some undisclosed information.

A more recent Irish case that looked at these issues was *Geoghegan v Harris* [2000] 3 IR 536.

Facts: The patient underwent a dental implant procedure. As a result of a bone graft taken from his chin in the course of the procedure, the patient suffered damage to the incisive nerve at the front of his chin, which, from the time of the procedure, left him with a condition of severe pain at the mid line of his chin known as chronic neuropathic pain. It was accepted by both plaintiff and defendant that the bone graft, rather than the insertion of the dental implants, was the cause of this pain.

The patient sued the surgeon for failing to disclose to him in advance of the operation that there was a risk that he might suffer chronic pain as a consequence of the procedure. The defendant surgeon argued that the risk of this occurring was less than one per cent and he did not think it necessary to disclose this risk. The plaintiff responded to this argument by stating that he would not have consented to the operation if he had known of the risk, however small.

Issue before the court: Should the defendant have disclosed the risk of the pain, despite the improbability of it occurring?

Decision of the court: The court held that whether a risk is material will be determined by the severity of the consequences should the risk materialise and the statistical frequency of that risk. The court thereafter adopted the position that is more commonly used in deciding causation in negligence cases and held that the plaintiff was required to show the court that he would not have consented to the procedure if the risk had been disclosed. The court accepted that the patient had been very eager to proceed with the implant and it was not convinced that the patient would not have proceeded if told of the risk. The plaintiff therefore failed in his claim.

The court adopted the objective reasonable patient test, along the lines of *Canterbury* (and also the Canadian case of *Riebl v Hughes* (1980) 114 DLR (3d) 1 (SC)). At the same time the court attempted to solve the problems inherent in the *Canterbury* approach by adopting what is essentially a causation test. What this means is that it is not enough to show that the medical practitioner did not disclose the risk; plaintiffs need to go further and show that they would not have agreed to the procedure if they had known of the risk. It is not enough to just assert this – it is clear that by suing the doctor the plaintiff is asserting this – plaintiffs must prove on a balance of probabilities that they would not have agreed to the procedure if the risk had been disclosed.

The decision is useful in that it clearly establishes a duty on the doctor to disclose material risks (in elective treatment) but at the same time recognises that the *Walsh* decision is unworkable in practice as it requires disclosure of all and any risk where the procedure is deemed to be elective, as this one was. In an attempt to circumvent the *Walsh* defect, the court continued to establish the right of the patient to choose whether to proceed with the treatment.

The court in *Geoghegan* therefore chose what was essentially a reasonable patient test, but at the same time placed the burden of proof on the plaintiff to show he would not have consented to the procedure had he known of the undisclosed risk, the inference being that where a risk is known to be extremely remote (less than one per cent probability of occurring) the reasonable patient would choose to proceed.

The decision has been criticised for placing a great burden on plaintiff-patients to prove that they would not have agreed to a procedure if the risk had been disclosed. This might be a difficult requirement and in practice the court will probably be led by the magnitude of the risk. If a patient is told that there is a less than one per cent chance of the harm occurring, it is likely that this will not cause the reasonable or average patient to refuse the treatment. On the other hand, where the risk is described as being a real possibility, many patients might have second thoughts. The most problematic situations are where the risk is very small, but the consequences are drastic. The courts may have difficulty in deciding such cases.

The court also made it clear that it would take evidence concerning the events leading up to the consent being given, including more subjective factors such as the patient's behaviour and prior statements, and in that way attempt to assess the state of mind of the patient and his or her eagerness to have the treatment or procedure. After looking at this bigger picture, the court would be in a better position to decide whether a disclosure of the risk would have caused the patient to change his or her mind.

Geoghegan was a High Court decision and, despite being highly influential, was not binding on the Supreme Court, where *Walsh*, with all its practical difficulties, remained the leading Irish decision on the question of disclosure of material risk. This situation was remedied to some extent by the Supreme Court in its judgment of *Fitzpatrick v Royal Victoria Eye & Ear Hospital* [2007] IESC 51.

Facts: The patient underwent corrective surgery for a serious squint. Although the original surgery improved the situation markedly, the patient decided to undergo further surgery to correct the squint. The surgeon warned the patient, thirty minutes before the operation, that there were risks associated with the proposed surgery. The surgery was then carried out competently and there was no question of negligence. However, due to an existing condition, the patient thereafter suffered from double vision and headaches.

Issue before the court: Had there been sufficient disclosure of the material risks, particularly in view of the fact that these were raised half an hour before the operation was due to commence?

Decision of the court: The Supreme Court confirmed the principles laid down in *Geoghegan*. On the facts, the court held that the disclosure was adequate. The plaintiff therefore failed in his claim. However, as the scope of the appeal was very narrow and considered the timing of the warning given by the surgeon rather than the content of that warning, Kearns J was unable to throw out of Irish law the strict requirement of disclosure in elective surgery, which still remains part of the law, despite being recognised as unworkable in practice.

Kearns J concluded by saying that the surgeon had a duty to reveal 'material and significant' risks, although he seemed to regard those two words as interchangeable. Essentially this is the test of the reasonable patient:

> As I stressed in *Geoghegan v Harris*: 'The reasonable man, entitled as he must be to full information of material risks, does not have impossible expectations nor does he seek to impose impossible standards. He does not invoke only the wisdom of hindsight if things go wrong. He must be taken as needing medical practitioners to deliver on their medical expertise without excessive restraint or gross limitation on their ability to do so.'

Determining What the Patient Wants to Know

The traditional or paternalistic approach, whereby health professionals told patients only what health professionals were prepared to tell patients, is clearly untenable today. At the same time, the 'tell all' approach can be criticised as being impractical and idealistic as health professionals cannot always guess what it is that patients want to know or what they would consider important. In the busy world of medicine, where practitioners rarely have the opportunity to get to know their patients very well, this is a credible argument. The other argument that might be raised against the 'tell all' approach is that patients are often under stress, and possibly mental anguish, and an information-overload may exacerbate any confusion, rather than offer clarification.

The Irish courts have adopted a position somewhere in the middle of these two extremes. Patients have the right to know all material and significant risks, particularly if the procedure is elective as opposed to therapeutic, but at the same time patients must show that consent would have been withdrawn or withheld if they had been told of the particular risk that subsequently materialised.

Practical Implications of the Law Relating to Disclosure

What does all this mean in practice? First, health professionals must realise that patients are usually ordinary people and want to know the things that ordinary people want to know. These would run along the lines of:

- What are the chances of success?
- Are there any serious risks involved?
- Are there any alternatives?
- Is it going to be very expensive?
- Have you done many of these before?
- Does it have to be done now or can I think about it a little longer?
- Do you think it is necessary?
- Can you think of anybody else that I should talk to?

These questions can be answered in ordinary everyday language as they are ordinary everyday questions. If doctors contemplated and prepared the answers to these questions before doing their rounds, it might be possible to put a lot more patients at ease in a relatively short time, rather than either attempting to avoid the whole process or being evasive in answering questions.

People who claim that the concept of informed consent is idealistic and impractical are assuming that a patient wants to know everything about anything. This is not true and the practice of informing patients should not be dismissed on that false premise.

The nurse can play an important role in this question-and-answer exercise by finding out the questions beforehand. Through frequent contact with the patient, the nurse could soon discover the questions the patient would like to ask but has not, could not or will not ask. Again, rather than go through the time-consuming process of getting over these hurdles, a doctor who has been briefed in advance by a nurse could answer these questions in a considerably shorter period.

Doctors need to keep careful notes detailing consultations with patients. They should record the questions asked by a patient and the patient's responses to the answers to these questions and other information relating to risks. Nurses would do well to keep a similar record of the questions asked by the patient. Not only could they thereafter hand these questions over to the doctor or surgeon to assist the doctor in properly informing the patient, but this would also ensure that the nurse has an independent record of a patient's questions and concerns. This could be crucial evidence regarding the state of mind of the patient if the matter later went to court.

Informed consent is really a form of honest-to-goodness communication and one does not need the law to make that possible. It is a practical matter concerning common sense more than anything else.

The benefits of disclosure are not only for the patient

If a doctor obtains the consent of the patient, an action for battery cannot lie against that doctor if the operation is not a success. Full disclosure further protects the doctor as the patient made the choice of treatment after being properly informed. Accordingly, if the operation is not a success, the patient is responsible for the decision and cannot argue that he or she would have chosen another procedure. In fact the patient did choose that procedure and only after being properly briefed. The law will never allow unjustified wisdom after the event where the patient was properly involved in the decision leading to that event.

If a doctor performs his or her job competently and to the required standard of care after answering the types of question previously discussed, then that doctor is effectively immune from being found liable under tort. In addition, there are the obvious therapeutic advantages of joint decision making. Accordingly, the nurse can be seen as a doctor advocate as well as a patient advocate by facilitating the process leading to the disclosure to the patient.

Disclosure is about empowerment

More often than not patients are going to consent to the procedure as they would not be in hospital in the first place if they were opposed to having treatment. Proper disclosure is not about getting patients to agree to a treatment or a procedure in instances where they would usually refuse. Proper disclosure is about giving patients more autonomy. If patients are aware of the attendant risks, they may ask for a second opinion or employ the services of a more experienced or skilled surgeon, which is their way of attempting to minimise those risks. If patients do not know about the risks, they are not able to avail of these options. Therefore disclosure is about autonomy and empowerment, rather than about changing a person's mind.

Doctors might argue that they did not tell a patient about the risks as this would have frightened the patient away, thus preventing that patient from receiving necessary treatment. This is paternalism as it assumes that patients will flee at the first sign of danger, which is usually not the case. Patients have often already been through that internal conflict before admitting themselves to hospital and it is unlikely that, when told of a risk with a less than one per cent chance of occurring, they will have a change of heart.

When the practice of disclosure becomes an established part of a health professional's mode of operation it benefits both patients and health professionals, and indeed the health service as a whole. As previously discussed, the nurse has a crucial role in ensuring its successful implementation.

Therapeutic Privilege

The issue of therapeutic privilege was considered in *Canterbury*, where it was stated that if a patient is likely to become distraught by the disclosure of medical information and this distress will cause the patient to become incapable of making an informed decision, then information may be kept from the patient by the doctor.

In *Sidaway*, the practice was accepted as being necessary in certain situations, but the court stressed that the burden of proof was on the doctor to show that concealment was necessary and justified. 'There is a need that the doctor should have the opportunity of proving that he reasonably believed that disclosure of the risk would be damaging to his patient or contrary to his best interests.'

This approach can be criticised for a number of reasons. First, it is formulated very widely – 'best interests of the patient' can be interpreted in a number of ways. Would it not be better to restrict its application to instances of clearly foreseeable harm or damage to the patient? If not, it is possible for a doctor to use the 'privilege' to avoid telling a patient about the risks on the basis that they think it is in that patient's best interests to have the treatment. This is, after all, why most of the problems arise: a doctor thinks that a patient will necessarily refuse the treatment when told of the risks. As has been argued before, this view is probably far from the truth.

Second, when it was used in *Canterbury* the court was dealing with the concept as a capacity issue. In other words, the doctor can withhold information only where the patient's capacity to make an informed decision would be lost if the risk was made known to the patient. This is a far narrower test than the 'best interests' test.

The notion of therapeutic privilege can be condemned as being paternalistic in the extreme. The example usually given to justify therapeutic privilege is when a person has a terminal illness and the relatives have asked that the patient not be informed. This situation is fraught with both ethical and legal problems. From an ethical point of view, it is insulting and demeaning to a patient if he or she is considered incapable of handling the news of imminent death. From a legal point of view, it means that confidentiality has been breached as the relatives should be told the condition of the patient only with the consent of that patient. As the patient has been kept in the dark, clearly he or she could not have consented to the disclosure being made to the family.

Remember that privileged information is information that a person can prevent from being led as evidence in court and in tort a person cannot be sued for defaming somebody on certain privileged occasions. It is puzzling that therapeutic privilege has nothing to do with either of those things; indeed, it is unclear why it has been called a 'privilege' at all. The 'privilege' belongs to the medical professional who claims that he or she cannot be forced to disclose bad news.

The concept of therapeutic privilege does not seem to have gained a foothold in Irish law and it is unlikely that any court today would accept it.

Nurses and therapeutic privilege

Nurses often find themselves in an impossible position in these kinds of situation. They are obliged (usually under threat of disciplinary proceedings) to obey a doctor's instructions not to inform a patient of his or her condition, and yet at the same time their daily contact with the patient in question may force them to lie if asked a direct question. The nurse in such a position must obey the doctor's instruction, and if the patient does ask a direct question, the nurse should summon the doctor immediately and allow him or her to answer the patient. The fact that the nurse evades the question and summons the doctor should indicate to the patient that something is not right and therefore the doctor is likely to face a barrage of questions from the patient. This, of course, assumes that the doctor is available to respond to the nurse's call.

Nurses would do well to inform doctors that the concept of therapeutic privilege is riddled with ethical and legal problems and that doctors would be well advised to avoid such a practice. Recent experiences with AIDS patients have shown that patients are often more positive once told of their illness; as with any illness, uncertainty is more crippling than the truth.

Full and proper disclosure: summary

1   The patient-oriented approach to disclosure is based on what the patient thinks is a material risk. This can place the medical practitioner in an impossible position as he or she is expected to know what a patient would consider important.

2   The doctor-oriented approach to disclosure is based on what the medical profession as a whole thinks should be disclosed. This can lead to paternalism and excludes the patient from the decision-making process, which is itself an important aspect of the therapeutic process. It also means that the courts must surrender to the opinions of the medical profession.

3   The Irish courts have attempted to steer a middle course between these two extremes. It is the court and not the medical profession (nor the patient) that must ultimately decide whether there was sufficient disclosure.

4   Although the Irish courts have used an approach that is similar to the reasonable patient test, the important difference is that patients must show that they would not have consented to the treatment or procedure if they had been aware of the risk in question. This causative requirement lessens the burden placed on the medical practitioner by the patient-oriented approach, but at the same time makes it clear that the patient must be properly informed of all material risks.

Further reading

Burns, P., Keogh, I. and Timon, C. 'Informed consent: a patient's perspective', *The Journal of Laryngology & Otology* 119 (2005), 19–22.

Healy, J. 'Failure of doctors to communicate risks to patients at the pre-treatment stage: a case of negligence or medical negligence? Part I', *Irish Law Times* 13 (1995), 196.

Healy, J. 'Failure of doctors to communicate risks to patients at the pre-treatment stage: a case of negligence or medical negligence? Part II', *Irish Law Times* 13 (1995), 222.

Healy, J. 'Informed consent to medical treatment: a case of medical negligence', *Dublin University Law Journal* 4/1 (1997), 178.

Heywood, R. 'Medical disclosure of alternative treatments', *Cambridge Law Journal* 68/1 (2009), 30–32.

Li, J.-Y., Liu, C., Zou, L.-Q., Huang, M.-J., Yu, C.-H., You, G.-Y., Jiang, Y.-D., Li, H. and Jiang, Y. 'To tell or not to tell: attitudes of Chinese oncology nurses towards truth telling of cancer diagnosis', *Journal of Clinical Nursing* 17 (2008), 2463–70.

Jones, M. A. 'Informed consent and other fairy stories', *Medical Law Review* 7 (1999), 103–34.

Kendall, S. 'Being asked not to tell: nurses' experiences of caring for cancer patients not told their diagnosis', *Journal of Clinical Nursing* 15 (2006), 1149–57.

Miola, J. 'On the materiality of risk: paper tigers and panaceas', *Medical Law Review* 17 (2009), 76–108.

Moore, R. A., Derry, S., McQuay, H. J. and Paling, J. 'What do we know about communicating risk? A brief review and suggestion for contextualising serious, but rare, risk, and the example of cox-2 selective and non-selective NSAIDs', *Arthritis Research & Therapy* 10/1 (2008), R20.

Shannon, H. and Scott, T. 'Patients' perceptions of informed consent for surgical procedures in Northern Ireland: a retrospective survey', *British Journal of Anaesthetic & Recovery Nursing* 9/3 (2008), 55–65.

Useful websites

Medical Council: www.medicalcouncil.ie

Patient Focus: www.patientfocus.ie

VOLUNTARY CONSENT

Introduction

The fact that a patient has sufficient information to make an informed decision concerning the acceptance or refusal of medical treatment is meaningless if the patient is not given the freedom to make up his or her own mind on the matter.

While cases of involuntary or forced treatment are obviously outside the bounds of what is accepted as consensual treatment, the question of consent to treatment in a formalised institution such as a hospital, and the corresponding question of whether patients are properly advised of their right to refuse treatment, are much thornier issues with no clear answers. There is a fine line between advising and instructing when it comes to a person in a position of authority and power communicating with a patient. The manner of presenting advice and information can have a profound influence on a patient, with the question of manipulation of information and emotions adding further complexity.

The Notion of Voluntariness

Voluntariness as a concept is often difficult to explain as it is usually defined in relation to the absence of other factors. In other words, a person's conduct is regarded as voluntary when there is an absence of coercion, duress or control. Duress and undue influence are very similar concepts and are really separated by degree rather than meaning. Duress involves the threat of bodily injury or violence (a physical threat) whereas undue influence involves psychological pressure or even blackmail (an emotional threat). It is sometimes difficult to distinguish between the two and therefore they will be considered together for the purposes of this chapter.

As there are no reported decisions concerning duress and undue influence in the health care sector, it is necessary to look elsewhere in the law in an effort to understand these concepts properly. An area where duress and undue influence are often considered is the law of marriage, and more specifically the law of nullity, where the allegation is made that a valid marriage was never entered into because of some nullifying factor. The most obvious example of a marriage under duress is the so-called 'shotgun marriage', but the examples in the reported cases are usually a little more sophisticated.

The leading Irish case in this area is the Supreme Court decision of *N (otherwise K) v K* [1986] 6 ILRM 75.

Facts: The nineteen-year-old bride claimed that her father had forced her to marry when it was discovered that she was pregnant. Her evidence was that her father had given her the option of marriage or an abortion.

Issue before the court: Was the choice of marriage or abortion a real choice or did the bride feel that she had no choice but to marry?

Decision of the court: The Supreme Court held that consent to marriage must be a full and free exercise of the independent will of the parties. Consent must be real, not just apparent. The court held that it did not matter whether the external pressure was proper or improper, legal or illegal, what was important was that the pressure was enough to remove the free exercise of will. McCarthy J defined this consent as 'a true voluntary consent based upon adequate knowledge and freed from vitiating factors commonly described as undue influence or duress, particularly those emanating from third parties'.

Another potentially relevant case involving marriage and true consent is the Supreme Court decision in *B v O'R* [1991] 1 IR 289.

Facts: The wife had been raised in a convent until she left at the age of fifteen. She had sexual intercourse with a man aged twenty-six and fell pregnant. When her parents discovered her pregnancy they sent her back to the convent. The nun in charge of the convent contacted the man and arranged for them to be married. The girl took part in the marriage ceremony but the evidence was that she was in a dazed state at the time and did not truly comprehend what was going on.

Issue before the court: Although nobody had forced the girl to marry (as in the previous case), could it be said that she had voluntarily consented to the marriage?

Decision of the court: The Supreme Court found that the pressure to marry had not come from a person but was rather created by the situation in which the girl found herself. This pressure of circumstance was enough to rob the girl of her capacity to consent as it was not possible in those circumstances for the girl to exercise free will.

On reading the *N v K* judgment, it is important to notice that the Supreme Court adopted a subjective approach to the question of voluntary consent. It considered whether the person in question felt that she had the freedom of choice, as opposed to what a reasonable person would have thought in the circumstances. This has important implications for the question of patient consent.

Although the test for disclosure is essentially an objective test, it might be argued that the test for voluntariness should be a subjective one: did the patient in question feel that he or she had the right to refuse treatment or demand alternative treatment? Of course, as in all subjective tests, the court will not just take the word of the patient as the absolute truth, it will also look at the behaviour of the patient at the time of consent and hear evidence as to what the patient said or asked at the time that consent was sought. The court will try to determine the state of mind of the patient by the way he or she was acting at the time. What is important, however, is that the court will be looking at the question from the patient's point of view when deciding whether there was an exercise of free will by the patient.

The phrasing of advice

When health professionals speak to patients in order to obtain consent, the phrasing of advice and the tenor of questions and answers very often create the impression that the only possible option available to the patient is to consent to the treatment offered. Or when alternative treatments are offered, a patient may be made to think that it is imperative to choose either a particular one or at least one. It seldom occurs in practice that a health professional offers a patient the choice of refusal.

Indeed, it has been strongly argued that a health professional is under an ethical duty to attempt to persuade the patient to accept a suggested treatment as the health professional has the expertise and qualifications to understand, better than most, the advantages of receiving that treatment. The argument continues that if a health professional is not allowed to attempt to persuade the patient as to the best treatment, then that professional is simply a technician, being reactive rather than proactive. This is a compelling argument, but it will always be a question of degree: when does persuasion become compulsion?

In summary, it must be argued that if one is to adopt a truly subjective test on the issue of voluntariness, the health professional should be careful to explain the options available, including the right to refuse any treatment and the probable consequences of that refusal. If a patient is not offered all the available options, it can hardly be said to be a subjective test of voluntariness because the patient is not given the freedom of choice. At most the patient has a restricted choice, and in many instances no choice at all.

A scenario that nurses are likely to encounter is terminally ill or elderly patients who want to 'go home to die' rather than spending their last days in a hospital ward in a strange bed. If the principle of voluntariness was upheld, such patients should be allowed to leave immediately, assuming that they do not pose any danger to society (for example, if they have a notifiable or contagious disease). It is in situations like this that the nurse can truly be a patient advocate. A doctor cannot lawfully order a patient to remain in hospital if that patient wants to leave, unless that patient is incapacitated and unable to make that decision or poses some threat to society. The competent patient who wants to leave should be allowed to do so and the nurse should inform the patient of that right.

Institutionalisation

In the *B v O'R* judgment, a subjective test was used and in addition it was recognised that the pressure can be created by events or by a situation and does not need to come from another person. This might be relevant to the question of a patient ostensibly consenting to treatment in an institutionalised setting. Patients in a hospital may get used to the idea of people telling them what to do: when to wake up, when to eat, what to eat, when to take their medicine, when to take a bath and so on. They may also experience a feeling of helplessness. Patients in such a frame of mind may not realise that they are being offered a choice as they are so used to doing as they are told. Once again, the nurse has a crucial role to play in ensuring that patients are aware that consent to treatment involves choice and that this choice should include alternative treatments or no treatment at all.

Education is a crucial element of free choice

It is necessary at this point to distinguish between education and undue influence. Doctors and even nurses routinely recommend certain types of treatment or procedures to patients. What is important is how these recommendations are phrased. The patient must be made fully aware that what is being suggested is one of a number of choices, including the right to refuse treatment altogether. If the patient is not properly informed (educated) about all the choices available, then it cannot be said that the patient has freedom of choice.

As mentioned earlier, doctors and nurses are trained to save lives or at least to make patients' lives more comfortable. It goes against their training to allow a person to die. However, the concept of informed consent and the element of voluntariness would be meaningless if that right to refuse treatment was not recognised and respected. The doctor and nurse can provide the patient with choice, they can educate the patient about the available choices, they can even recommend what choice to make, but they cannot make the choice. The choice must be left to the patient.

Voluntariness: summary

1 Voluntariness is a state of mind. The patient must feel that he or she can exercise free will.

2 Duress and undue influence can deprive a patient of his or her free will.

3 Although duress will usually come from another person and is not likely to occur in the health care context (at least where consent is required), undue influence can also arise from a situation or setting.

4 An institutionalised setting such as a hospital can create an environment where a patient loses sight of the fact that he or she has the right to choose. It is the duty of the health professional, in particular the nurse, to remind the patient of this right to free will.

5 The education of the patient is an important part of voluntariness. The patient cannot be said to exercise free will if that will is curtailed by the choices on offer.

6 Advice should never go further than a reasoned recommendation. The final choice must be made by the patient.

7 The freedom to consent to medical treatment includes the freedom to refuse treatment or to choose an alternative treatment.

Further reading

Chamberlain-Webber, J. 'Nursing's role in patient choice', *Professional Nurse* 20 (2005), 18–22.

Guo, F. 'A concept analysis of voluntary active euthanasia', *Nursing Forum* 41 (2006), 167–71.

Harvath, T. A., Miller, L. L., Goy, E., Jackson, A., Delorit, M. and Ganzini, L. 'Voluntary refusal of food and fluids', *International Journal of Palliative Nursing* 10 (2004), 236–41.

Lind, M., Kaltiala-Heino, R., Suominen, T., Leino-Kilpi, H. and Valimaki, M. 'Nurses' ethical perceptions about coercion', *Journal of Psychiatric and Mental Health Nursing* 11 (2004), 379–85.

O'Neill, C. 'Nurses' ethical decisions in the medical world', *Medico-Legal Journal of Ireland* 3/2 (1997), 73.

Quinn, M. J. 'Undoing undue influence', *Generations* 24 (2000), 65–9.

Sheppard, C. 'Helping patients choose', *Cancer Nursing Practice* 7 (2008), 18–20.

Slater, L. 'Palliative care: do all patients now have a choice about where they die?', *Nursing Times* 106/7 (2010), 20–22.

Sørgaard, K. W. 'Satisfaction and coercion among voluntary, persuaded/pressured and committed patients in acute psychiatric treatment', *Scandinavian Journal of Caring Sciences* 21 (2007), 214–19.

Staunton, C. 'The development of health care planning in Ireland', *Medico-Legal Journal of Ireland* 15/2 (2009), 74.

Useful websites

Lenus, The Irish Health Repository: www.lenus.ie/hse

Dementia Services Information and Development Centre: www.dementia.ie

WorldWideScience.org: www.worldwidescience.org

Somerset Partnership (UK): www.sompar.nhs.uk

Psychiatric Patient Advocate Office (Canada): www.ppao.gov.on.ca

Part 3

CRIMINAL LIABILITY

chapter 11

BASIC CONCEPTS IN CRIMINAL LAW

> *Learning outcomes*
> At the completion of this chapter the reader should know and understand:
> * The concepts of *actus reus* and *mens rea*.
> * The distinction between the notions of direct intention, recklessness and negligence as they apply to criminal law.
> * Common defences in criminal law.

Actus Reus and *Mens Rea*

In simple terms, a criminal offence can be described as having a physical element and a mental element.

A crime must always consist of an unlawful (physical) act. Without the unlawful act, or *actus reus* (Latin for 'wrongful act'), there can never be a crime. You cannot be punished for your thoughts alone. An act does not have to be a positive action in order to be an *actus reus*. It can also be a failure to do something. For example, a driver who fails to stop a vehicle when somebody is using the pedestrian crossing. A failure to do something is called an omission.

In exceptional circumstances a mere condition or state of affairs is punishable. For example, it is a statutory crime to be drunk in certain public places or to be in possession of certain illegal substances. In other words, it is the conduct itself that is being punished. These are known as 'strict liability' crimes, as they do not require proof of an intention to break the law.

The act must be linked directly (attributable) to the defendant and not to another person or thing. If the act was committed by a person other than the defendant, the defendant can only be held responsible for that act if he or she incited (persuaded) the other person to do it, or if he or she was acting with a common purpose with that other person (an accomplice). A person can be held liable if he or she acts through the agency of an animal, which is what happens when the animal commits the wrongful act while under the control of the person. For example, if a person instructs his or her dog to bite somebody, the dog owner may be liable for a crime, even though he or she did not lay a finger on the victim.

The act must be done voluntarily by the defendant. It must be an act over which the human will exercises control. Therefore the actions of a person carried out whilst asleep or unconscious or during an epileptic attack do not fall into the category of unlawful acts.

Mens rea means a blameworthy state of mind, or a guilty mind. While some people often say that *mens rea* is wrongful intent, this is not accurate as there are some crimes that do not require specific intent, as will be seen later. It is better to think of *mens rea* as a wrongful state of mind.

As it is usually impossible to prove the guilty mind of an accused person, the law often presumes or deduces a guilty mind from the actions of the accused person. For example, if a person drives at high speed down the wrong side of the road on a dual carriageway and causes the death of another, then that would be manslaughter as the driver was so negligent as to be considered to be acting in a way that there was a reckless disregard of danger to the health and welfare of the victim.

What the law regards as blameworthy varies from offence to offence. The 'purest' form of *mens rea* is where the conduct is intentional. What this means is that the defendant intended to perform the wrongful act, and intended to perform the wrongful act in order to cause something to happen. The consequence of the intended action was not only foreseen by the defendant, it was desired by the defendant. Crimes requiring intention are the most serious crimes, for example murder. With murder, the defendant must foresee and desire the death of the victim at the same time as causing the death.

Mens rea may also be in the form of recklessness. This is where the defendant committed the unlawful act and at the time was conscious of the danger but did not care whether it would occur, even though he or she did not directly desire the results of that act. A well-known crime of recklessness is manslaughter. Recklessness is a difficult concept to understand as it depends on whether the test is subjective or objective. The subjective test would be that a person is reckless if that person consciously took an unjustified risk about which he or she already knew. The objective test says that a person is reckless if he or she consciously took an unjustified risk about which the person did not know but of which he or she ought to have been aware. The Irish courts traditionally favoured the subjective test, while in England the law seems to be drifting towards the stricter objective test. Recent decisions blur this distinction.

Finally, *mens rea* may be in the form of negligence. Here the defendant intends to commit the wrongful conduct, but does not foresee the consequences of that conduct in a situation where he or she ought to have foreseen the consequences. This is very similar to the civil concept of negligence, namely behaviour falling below an accepted standard of conduct.

It is sometimes very difficult to distinguish recklessness from negligence as it would seem that the two concepts are separated by a matter of degree rather than by a fundamental difference of meaning. With recklessness, the law seems to be saying 'you must have seen the risk, but carried on anyway', whereas with negligence the law seems to be saying 'you should have seen the risk before you did what you did'. Recklessness will not be lightly inferred from the type of evidence that would justify a finding of negligence.

Motive

A common mistake is to confuse *mens rea* with motive. This may be a result of too many television shows where the detective talks about 'means, motive and opportunity' as the unholy triad of crime solving. It works for script writers, but it is not the law. A person's motive for committing a crime is largely irrelevant as far as the necessary ingredients for a crime are concerned. A person who steals from the rich at gunpoint and distributes the money to the poor may have the purest of motives, but it does not mean that he or she is not guilty of armed robbery. The necessary *actus reus* and *mens rea* are present and so the legal definition of a crime is satisfied. Robin Hood goes to jail for a very serious offence.

Defences

Whilst there are a number of general defences to a criminal charge, namely infancy, insanity, intoxication, duress, self-defence and necessity, it is unlikely that a nurse will be able to avail of most of these if he or she is charged with a crime arising out of the performance of the nurse's professional duties. One defence that might be used where a nurse commits a crime arising out of the performance of professional duties, depending on the circumstances, will be that of necessity.

Necessity

The defence of necessity in criminal law is virtually identical, at least in principle, to the one in tort. Where a defendant commits a lesser evil in order to avoid a greater evil, the defendant can plead the defence of necessity if the lesser evil is a criminal offence. For example, a person pulls a drowning boy out of the river but in so doing breaks the victim's collar bone. In response to a charge of (statutory) assault, the defendant can lead evidence that the child was drowning and would have died if he had not been pulled out of the river.

In criminal law the defence of necessity is limited in its use:

- It cannot be used as a defence to murder. For policy reasons, and for the same reasons that duress is not a defence to murder, a person cannot argue that he killed one (faultless) person in order to save the life of another (faultless) person. This would leave the court with an impossible task of deciding whether one person's life is more valuable than the other's.
- The defendant needs to show that there was no alternative action available to take at the time. The defendant must show that the only reasonable way he or she could avoid the greater evil was to commit the crime that is the basis of the criminal charge. A health care example would be where a nurse responds to a patient's call and discovers that the patient is having difficulty breathing. The nurse administers aggressive CPR, causing severe bruising to the chest and much pain to the patient. The patient lays a charge of (statutory) assault. The nurse pleads necessity but it is shown that an oxygen canister and mask were next to the bed and would have been more than adequate to help the patient to breathe. The court might decide on those facts

that the defence of necessity should fail as the use of CPR was not the only option available to the nurse.

- The defendant must show that in committing the lesser evil he or she did no more than was necessary at the time. Again, the defendant must do enough to prevent the greater evil, but no more than that. Taking the previous example of the nurse who used CPR on a patient having difficulty breathing, although this time the oxygen was not available, if it is shown that the use of aggressive CPR was not justified as the problem could easily have been solved by mouth-to-mouth resuscitation, the nurse might again fail on the defence of necessity as he or she went further than was necessary.

- The defendant must show that he or she did not create the situation that necessitated breaking the law. Clearly the defendant cannot justify committing the lesser evil if he or she was the cause of the greater evil in the first place. In the previous example, if the nurse was somehow responsible for the patient not breathing, then the nurse cannot rely on necessity to justify his or her subsequent actions.

Basic concepts of criminal law: summary

1 *Actus reus* means an act forbidden by law. The act can be a positive form of conduct (a commission) or a failure to do something where there was a legal duty to do it (an omission). The act must be done by the defendant personally or by someone who is incited by the defendant, is acting in concert with the defendant or is under the control of the defendant. The act must be voluntary.

2 *Mens rea* means a blameworthy state of mind or a guilty mind. What the law regards as blameworthy varies from offence to offence. It may be intentional wrongdoing as in murder or rape, where the consequences are foreseen and desired. It may be reckless wrongdoing as in manslaughter, where the consequences are foreseen but not necessarily desired at the time of taking the risk. It may be negligent wrongdoing as in dangerous driving, where the consequences are not foreseen in circumstances where the law requires foresight.

3 The defence that is most likely to be used where a nurse is charged with a crime arising out of the performance of his or her professional duties is that of necessity, where the nurse will argue that he or she was forced to commit a crime on the patient in order to avoid a greater evil befalling that patient.

Further reading

Cady, R. C. 'Criminal prosecution for nursing errors', *JONA's Healthcare Law, Ethics, and Regulation* 11 (2009), 10–16.

Dimond, B. 'Liability for death: manslaughter, murder and other criminal offences', *British Journal of Nursing* 13 (2004), 858–60.

Hanly, C. *An Introduction to Irish Criminal Law*, 2nd edition, Dublin: Gill & Macmillan, 2006.

Useful websites

An Garda Síochána: www.garda.ie
Human Rights in Ireland: www.humanrights.ie
Office of the Director of Public Prosecutions: www.dpp.ie

chapter 12

ASSAULT AND SYRINGE OFFENCES

> *Learning outcomes*
> At the completion of this chapter the reader should know and understand:
> - The statutory offence of assault as set out in the Non-Fatal Offences Against the Person Act 1997.
> - The similarities and differences between statutory assault and common law assault.
> - The range of syringe offences set out in the Non-Fatal Offences Against the Person Act and their applicability to nurses.

Introduction

It is very seldom that one reads or hears about a nurse being charged with an offence from an incident arising out of his or her duties, but it does happen. It is important for nurses to understand that many of the actions that they perform on patients as a matter of routine are only lawful with the consent of the patient. When that consent is not supplied, the threat of being sued is not the only danger that arises, there is also the danger of the patient lodging a criminal complaint.

Criminal law is a huge subject and this chapter will look only at specific offences that are more likely to arise in the nursing context. The subject of drugs will be dealt with in Chapter 13.

Non-Fatal Offences Against the Person Act 1997

The Non-Fatal Offences Against the Person Act 1997 abolished the common law offences of assault, battery and false imprisonment, and substituted statutory offences. In addition, the Act created new offences, namely syringe offences, threat, coercion and harassment, and endangerment, all of which were previously unknown to the common law. Finally, the Act codified the existing offences of poisoning, and kidnapping and abduction. This chapter considers two of the offences contained in the Act that might be relevant to the area of nursing, namely assault and syringe offences.

Assault

Sections 2, 3 and 4 of the 1997 Act cover assault, with each section contemplating a differing level of harm:

- Section 2: where a person feels threatened or afraid of impending violence but no physical contact occurs.
- Section 3: where a physical assault causes harm to a person.

- Section 4: where a person intentionally or recklessly causes serious harm to another person.

The Act defines harm as meaning 'harm to body or mind and includes pain and unconsciousness'. For the purposes of Section 4, 'serious harm' is defined as 'injury which creates a substantial risk of death or which causes serious disfigurement or substantial loss or impairment of the mobility of the body as a whole or of the function of any particular bodily member or organ'.

Prior to the 1997 Act common law assault was a psychological crime in that it was committed when the offender made the victim think that he or she was about to be attacked or harmed. Battery was the physical crime of touching somebody without consent and covered an entire spectrum of 'touching' from fondling to punching the victim. A person was charged with common assault, which was effectively a combination of assault and battery.

The Act has similarly combined assault and battery in Section 2, and a person is now guilty of statutory assault if he or she commits either of what used to be common law assault or battery.

The *actus reus* of the crime is the direct or indirect application of force or the causing of an impact upon the victim's body, or causing the victim to reasonably fear (objective test) the immediate infliction of such force or impact. Like the common law before it, the Act does not distinguish between a strong force and a mild force, and therefore any degree of force, no matter how slight, is covered by this offence, ranging from a brutal beating to a gentle caress. The apprehension of harm must be immediate or within a reasonably short period of time. It must also be objectively reasonable, which means the threat must be such that a reasonable person would apprehend violence. The Act also makes it clear that the assault must be without the consent of the victim.

The *mens rea* of the crime is either intention or recklessness (see Chapter 11). Therefore, as far as nurses are concerned, where a nurse touches or holds down a patient or administers treatment to a patient without that patient's consent, despite the patient being in a position to give or refuse consent, that nurse has committed a crime of statutory assault and could be charged in terms of Section 2 of the 1997 Act. In cases where the patient is unable to consent, the nurse is still guilty of statutory assault as there has been unauthorised touching. In these circumstances the nurse would need to rely on the defence of necessity or justification.

Sections 3 and 4 describe what is usually referred to as aggravated assault, the common law offence prior to the Act. There were various types of aggravated assault under the common law and the position was very confusing. The Act has simplified matters by having two categories of assault: assault causing harm (Section 3) and assault causing serious harm (Section 4). For the purposes of defining the *actus reus* of these two offences, 'harm' expressly includes psychological harm, whereas 'serious harm' is very specifically defined and is limited to serious physical injury. The *mens rea* for the crime would be either intention or recklessness.

Syringe offences

Syringes are extremely useful instruments in the field of medicine and nurses will be called upon to use them in carrying out their duties. Unfortunately, syringes can also be used as weapons. The idea of syringes being used as weapons is not new, but with the advent of blood-borne diseases such as HIV and hepatitis, the spectre of the blood-filled syringe has taken on a very sinister connotation. The 1997 Act seeks to cover situations where that threat is used for criminal purposes. It is important to know the specific offences created by the Act that involve the use of syringes.

For the purpose of these offences, the definition of a syringe includes the needle that might be attached to the syringe and also covers any sharp instrument capable of piercing skin and injecting blood or a blood-like substance.

Section 6(1) of the Act creates an offence that consists of two elements. First, injuring another person by piercing the skin of that person with a syringe or by threatening to do so. Second, the accused person must intend the victim to believe, or where it can be shown that in the circumstances it is likely that the victim did believe, that he or she would become infected with a disease as a result of the injury. The wording of the section is such that it could be argued that this offence would include using an empty syringe or a syringe filled with another substance that was not blood, where some quality of the syringe itself or of its contents was enough to cause a person to believe they were infected as a result of the stabbing or would be infected if the threat was carried out.

Section 6(2) again creates an offence consisting of two elements. The first makes it an offence to spray, pour or put blood or a blood-like substance on the victim, or to threaten to spray, pour or put blood or a blood-like substance on the victim, using a syringe. The second element is the same as Section 6(1), namely that the accused must do so with the intention to cause the victim to believe that he or she is or will be infected, or where the circumstances are such that it is likely that the victim will be caused to believe that he or she will become infected if the attack is carried out.

Section 6(3) refers to what is called transferred intent, where the offender means to harm one person but harms another instead. If a person intended to commit a crime described in Sections 6(1) or 6(2) but did not stab (or spray etc.) the person who was the intended victim, the offender can still be charged under Section 6(3) as if he or she had in fact intended the unlucky bystander to be the victim. This prevents an offender who admits to intending to commit a crime from escaping by showing that he or she got the wrong person by mistake. In order to satisfy Section 6(3), the prosecution also needs to show that the third-party victim actually believed that he or she was infected. The section does not say that the belief must be reasonable, it must simply exist.

Section 6(5) makes it an offence to stab a person with a contaminated syringe or to spray, pour or put contaminated blood on a victim, or to do any of these things to a third person whilst trying to commit the offence on the intended victim. This offence is different from the previous offences in that there must be an actual attack with contaminated blood (as opposed to a blood-like substance) or syringes. It is also the only subsection in Section 6 that specifically mentions the punishment of life imprisonment (and/or an unlimited fine). This is because intentionally infecting a person with HIV is tantamount to murder, although the victim might live for years after the offence. The *mens rea* for this crime is intention; recklessness would not suffice, again underlining the seriousness of the offence.

Section 7 makes it an offence to possess a syringe with the intention to cause or to threaten injury. Clearly the offender must be aware that he or she possesses the syringe, but the prosecution does not need to prove that the offender had a specific victim in mind. Section 7 will require intention (to possess and cause injury etc.) but it might be that possession of such a syringe could be enough to convince the court of intention to injure or threaten as well.

Section 8 creates two distinct offences involving the placing or abandoning of syringes in a place where they are likely to injure another person. Section 8(1) is the less serious of the two offences as it involves abandoning a syringe in any place in such a manner that it is likely to injure another and does injure or intimidate another. Section 8(2) involves the situation where a person intentionally disposes of a syringe in such a manner that it injures another person. There are three elements to this crime that the prosecution must prove: the accused intended to injure, there was in fact an injury and the syringe was in fact contaminated. Section 8(2) is looking at a potentially fatal situation and therefore the *mens rea* is intention and the maximum penalty is an unlimited fine and/or life imprisonment.

Section 8(3) is directly applicable to nurses as it excuses them from liability under Section 8(1) if they misplaced a syringe whilst lawfully performing medical, dental or veterinary procedures. Note that the nurse would have to be engaged in a lawful activity. However, if the nurse deliberately placed or abandoned the syringe with the intention that somebody be infected, then the fact that this was done during a lawful nursing activity shall not be an excuse as that offence is created by Section 8(2) and not Section 8(1).

Specific offences: summary

1   The Non-Fatal Offences Against the Person Act 1997 replaced the common law offences of assault and battery with a new offence of assault that is in essence a combination of the two common law offences.

2   The Act also created a number of syringe offences that penalise the use of a syringe to infect somebody or to threaten to infect somebody, either by stabbing that person with the syringe or leaving or placing the syringe somewhere so that a person is infected with the contents of the syringe, or where a syringe is used to spray or pour its contents over the victim so that the person is infected or thinks that he or she is infected.

3   Although one would hope that it is highly unlikely that a nurse would fall foul of these provisions whilst carrying out normal nursing duties such as disposing of used syringes, the seriousness of these offences and the severity of the punishments are a reminder to nurses that syringes and needles need to be handled with the utmost care and precaution.

Further reading

Byrne, R. 'The Non-Fatal Offences Against the Person Act', *Irish Law Times* 16 (1998), 245.

Useful websites

Seán Quinn (barrister): www.seanquinn.com

DRUGS

Introduction

Every nurse in every sector will at some stage in his or her career be asked to handle, control or administer drugs. These skills are an important part of any nurse's training. In addition, registered nurse prescribers are authorised to prescribe drugs. Drugs are clearly a huge asset to the health sector, but at the same time they are potentially lethal if misused or abused.

The Misuse of Drugs Act 1977, as amended by the Misuse of Drugs Act 1984, is the most important statute governing the regulation and administration of drugs. It is a very large and complex Act and this chapter will provide only a brief outline of its main features.

Another important statute is the Irish Medicines Board Act 1995. In terms of this Act, the Minister for Health and Children formulated the Medicinal Products (Prescription and Control of Supply) Regulations 2003, which, amongst other things, authorise the registered medical practitioner or dentist to prescribe medication.

More recently, the passing of the Irish Medicines Board (Miscellaneous Provisions) Act 2006 and the Medicinal Products (Prescription and Control of Supply) (Amendment) Regulations 2007 give legal authority to nurses and midwives to prescribe medications, as discussed in Chapter 3.

Misuse of Drugs Regulations 1988

From a practical point of view, the Regulations passed by the Minister for Health in terms of the Misuse of Drugs Acts are more useful than the Acts themselves, as they give the sort of information needed by somebody who has to deal with controlled drugs as part of their job. The principal Regulations are the Misuse of Drugs Regulations 1988, which replaced the 1979 Regulations and the 1987

Amendment Regulations. The 1988 Regulations have been updated by the Misuse of Drugs (Amendment) Regulations of 1993, 1999, 2006, 2007, 2009 and 2010. This is a very busy area of law and nurses are advised to keep up to date with the existing legislation. A detailed analysis of these Regulations/Orders is outside the scope of this book.

The 1988 Regulations are in four parts followed by six schedules. Part 1 is an introduction, which includes the important interpretation section. Part 2 deals with the production, supply, importation and exportation of controlled drugs, including Article 8 dealing with the supply of drugs in hospitals. Part 3 deals with documentation and record keeping, including Article 13 setting out the format and content of a valid prescription and Article 14 dealing with the supply of drugs in response to a prescription. Part 4 contains miscellaneous provisions, including details of the destruction and disposal of drugs and Article 24 dealing with the question of forged prescriptions. Finally, there are the schedules.

The schedules of controlled drugs

The drugs that are mentioned in the Regulations are known as controlled drugs, and these controlled drugs are sorted into five main categories or schedules.

Schedule 1 is a list of drugs in their raw form (i.e. before they are processed into pharmaceuticals). Well-known examples are cannabis and opium. Schedule 1 drugs can only be possessed under licence for research purposes by registered drug manufacturers and other State bodies conducting research.

Schedule 2 drugs are used for medicinal purposes but are dangerous in that they are either highly addictive or potentially toxic. Morphine and pethidine are two well-known examples of Schedule 2 drugs.

Schedule 3 drugs are used for medicinal purposes but are slightly 'softer' than Schedule 2 drugs in that they are usually in a more diluted form and often do not possess such toxic or highly addictive properties as Schedule 2 drugs. Well-known examples are Valium and a number of antibiotics.

Schedule 2 and 3 drugs are only available to patients on a prescription issued by a medical practitioner or dentist or veterinary surgeon (a vet, obviously, may only issue prescriptions for drugs for the purposes of treating an animal).

Schedule 4 drugs are 'over the counter' (as opposed to 'on the shelf') drugs that can be purchased in a pharmacy but are kept behind the counter and must be requested from the pharmacist. Examples are paracetamol and aspirin.

Schedule 5 drugs are drugs that may be imported or exported, examples of which are substances with codeine, ethylmorphine, nicocodine and nicodicodine as their base. As these substances contain opium bases, the schedule provides that they must be diluted or in a form that prevents extraction into their pure form so as to prevent them being used in a drug smuggling operation.

The Lawful Use of Drugs

Only certain people can possess and supply drugs. Nurses need to be very clear if and what drugs they are entitled to possess and/or supply as part of their job. But before considering what constitutes the lawful use of drugs, it is important to clarify certain terms that are often used in connection with drugs, which may or may not have a technical or specialised meaning in law. These concepts are 'possession', 'use', 'supply', 'dispense' and 'administer'.

Possession

The ordinary meaning of possession is the physical detention or keeping of something. In the legal sense, a person must not only physically possess something but must also have the intention to keep that thing as his or her own. Neither the Misuse of Drugs Act, as amended, nor the Regulations, as amended, specifically define possession, and therefore the ordinary meaning must be given to the concept when it is used in the Act or Regulations. As a general rule in the Act it is an offence to possess scheduled drugs unlawfully.

Although Section 1 (Interpretation) of the Act does not contain a specific definition of possession, it does make it clear that possession includes what is known as constructive possession: one person instructing another person to possess the drug on his or her behalf. In these circumstances the Act regards the person who issued the instruction as the possessor, even though he or she does not have physical possession.

The *actus reus* of illegal possession is actual (physical) or constructive possession. The *mens rea* of the offence is knowledge of the drug in question. The prosecution must prove that the defendant knew of the existence of the drug in his or her possession. The prosecution need only show that the defendant is in illegal possession of a controlled drug and that the defendant knew he or she was in possession of a controlled drug – irrespective of the type of drug. Section 29(1) of the Act says that if the accused was mistaken as to the type of controlled drug, such a mistake is not a defence if the possession of that drug is illegal.

Use

Again, the concept is not defined in the Act. The ordinary meaning of use is to employ or handle something for a purpose. In the legal sense, particularly with regard to drugs, the concept of use is equated with personal use. To possess a controlled drug illegally for personal use is less serious than possessing it for supply.

Supply

Again, the concept is not defined in the Act, with the interpretation section merely stating that 'supply' includes 'giving without payment'. Therefore the ordinary meaning of supply must be used. This meaning becomes very important as the distinction between use and supply is crucial. The ordinary meaning of supply is to provide something that is needed. If a person is convicted of illegal possession with intent to supply controlled drugs, as opposed to possession for personal use, the sentences that can be handed down to the convicted offender are a lot harsher.

It is difficult to prove that a person had an intention to supply and therefore the Act has created a presumption in Section 15. A rebuttable presumption of law allows the court to assume that something is a fact unless and until it is proven that it is not a fact. It is often referred to as a 'persuasive presumption'. If a person illegally possesses controlled drugs and the amount of drugs is more than seems necessary for personal use, then that person is presumed to be a supplier rather than a user. The evidential burden is then placed on the defendant to show that, despite the large quantity, the drugs were for personal use only. Evidence and argument will need to be led by the defendant to prove that.

Dispense

Again, the Act does not define this term. The ordinary meaning of dispense is to distribute or hand out.

Administer

Again, the Act does not define this term. The ordinary meaning is to give or furnish or apply. In the nursing context, to administer a drug usually means to dose the patient with the specific drug. In the legal sense, to administer a drug is in effect to supply a drug to another.

The supply of drugs

Where a supplier supplies a drug (as opposed to prescribing or administering a drug), Article 12 of the Misuse of Drugs Regulations 1988 provides that this shall only be on receipt of a written requisition, signed by the recipient of the drug and setting out the address and contact details of the recipient, the purpose for which the drug is to be used and the quantities required. If the drug is urgently needed and the requisition has not yet been obtained, then the supplier is entitled to supply the drug on an urgent basis with the stipulation that the requisition is supplied within twenty-four hours of the supplying of the drug.

If the person responsible for the dispensing and supply of medicines at any hospital or nursing home supplies a controlled drug to a sister/charge nurse in charge of a ward, theatre or other department in a hospital or nursing home, then that supplier must obtain a requisition in writing, signed by the sister/charge nurse, which specifies the total quantity of the drug to be supplied; and must mark the requisition in such manner as to show that it has been complied with. In these circumstances the requisition must be retained at the dispensary at which the drug was supplied and a copy of the requisition must be retained by the sister/charge nurse.

A person who supplies a controlled drug must provide a receipt with the consignment. The person who receives the consignment must check the receipt against the drugs supplied, note on that receipt any discrepancies between the contents of the receipt and the drugs received, enter the date on which the drugs were received, sign the receipt and return that receipt to the supplier not later than three working days after receiving the drugs.

Prescriptions

The supply of any 'prescription only' drugs must take place only if a valid prescription is produced. In the case of drugs governed by the Misuse of Drugs Regulations 1988, as amended, each product dispensed to a patient must be supplied only on receipt of a valid prescription written in accordance with the requirements specified in Article 13 of these Regulations. Article 13 of the 1988 Regulations was amended by the Misuse of Drugs (Amendment) Regulations 2007 to allow prescriptions by registered nurse prescribers.

Article 13 lays down the following requirements for a valid prescription of controlled drugs:

- The full name, qualifications and contact details of the prescribing practitioner (where practitioner is defined in Section 1 of the 1977 Act as 'a registered medical practitioner, a registered dentist, a registered veterinary surgeon, or, subject to article 3A, a registered nurse').
- It must be completed (i.e. the blank spaces must be filled in) in the handwriting of the practitioner concerned. The writing must be in ink and must be 'indelible', which means that it must be not be capable of being blotted out (at least not so it will not be noticed).
- It must be signed by the practitioner. The signature is not allowed to be a pre-printed signature, it must be an original signature in ink.
- It must contain the name and address of the patient for whom the drugs are prescribed.
- It must exactly specify the name and quantity of drugs prescribed (the quantity must be described in both words and figures).
- It must exactly specify the dose to be taken. Where the prescription is for a preparation of a controlled drug, it must specify the form and the strength of the preparation and either the total quantity (in both words and figures) of the preparation or the number (in both words and figures) of dosage units to be supplied.
- If the prescription is for a total quantity of drugs that are to be dispensed in instalments, it must contain a direction specifying the amount of the instalments and the intervals at which the instalments may be dispensed.

Clearly a prescription can only be in written form, which means that a prescription cannot be made over the telephone or in conversation. It must be in the form specified by Article 13.

Article 13 ends with an exception to these general rules, which is an important one for nurses to know: when dealing with a patient in a hospital or nursing home, it is sufficient if the prescription is written on the patient's bed card or case sheet.

It is a serious criminal offence either to forge a prescription or to alter a valid prescription with the intent to deceive. Pharmacists need to have faith in prescriptions and must be able to take them at face value. If there was widespread prescription forgery, the whole basis of trust would break down leading to chaos in the drug regulation system.

Recording of drugs

Article 16 of the 1988 Regulations deals with the keeping of a register for Schedule 1 and Schedule 2 drugs. Whenever a drug is administered a record must be kept of that administration in a register, recording who withdrew the drug and to whom it was administered, the quantity that was administered and when it was administered. The entries in the sections must be in chronological order and there must be a corresponding column next to the chronological entry to show a running stock balance. In other words, it must be possible to know from a reading of the register exactly how much of a particular drug is in stock at any one time. A register must be stored for a period of at least two years after the last entry in that register is made.

The creation and maintenance of such a register would usually have nothing to do with the nursing staff, but it is the duty of the nurse to ensure that when a patient is given a prescribed drug, that the drug is consumed in that nurse's presence and its consumption is thereafter recorded, usually on the patient's drug chart.

> *Drugs: summary*
> 1 The Misuse of Drugs Act 1977, as amended, is the primary statute concerning the regulation and administration of controlled (scheduled) drugs.
> 2 The Misuse of Drugs Regulations 1988, as amended, are equally important from a more practical point of view.
> 3 Contravention of the Act or the Regulations can lead to a criminal record, harsh punishments and almost certain dismissal.
> 4 An Bord Altranais (the Nursing Board) has issued guidelines on the regulation and administration of drugs. Courts are often guided by the principles contained in guidelines issued by professional bodies and therefore it is important that a nurse is familiar with these.

Further reading

An Bord Altranais *Medication Management: Guidance to Nurses and Midwives on Medication Management*, Dublin: An Bord Altranais, July 2007.

Useful websites

An Bord Altranais: www.nursingboard.ie
Drug and Alcohol Information and Support: www.drugs.ie
Irish Statute Book: www.irishstatutebook.ie

Part 4

ACCOUNTABILITY TO THE EMPLOYER

chapter 14

THE CONTRACT OF EMPLOYMENT

> *Learning outcomes*
> At the completion of this chapter the reader should know and understand:
> * The distinction between an employee and a self-employed person, and the implications of that distinction.
> * What should happen when an employee commences employment.
> * The main provisions of a number of statutes that protect employees.

Introduction

Although many do not realise the implications of being one, a lot of nurses are employees, usually of the Health Service Executive (HSE), but also of private hospitals or agencies. Employees in Ireland are protected by a whole host of laws. It is important for nurses to know their employment status and what laws are out there to protect them. However, it is also important to realise that not all people in employment are employees. By and large the labour laws protect only employees, which is why it is necessary to be certain of your status. Are you an employee or something else?

Employee or Self-Employed?

Those who work for others fall into two main categories:

* Employees who work under a contract of service.
* The self-employed (sometimes called independent contractors) who provide services under a contract.

There is another category of worker known as an office holder. This person has a position created by statute. The office holder's appointment, suspension, dismissal and remuneration are all determined by the statute, rather than by a contract. This category is relevant here as certain nurses might be held to be officers of a health board, in which event they are office holders in terms of the Health Act 1970. Such nurses are not employees and are therefore excluded from the protection of a number of statutes.

For the moment we will concentrate on the employee (contract of service) and the self-employed (contract for services).

An example can illustrate the differences between the two types of contract. Let us imagine that a home owner named Susan telephones a fencing contractor called Jack and asks him to come to her house and give her a quotation for a fence around the perimeter of her property. Jack does so and Susan accepts the quoted price. Susan and Jack have entered into a contract for services. Jack is not an employee of Susan; he has contracted with her to provide a service, namely the erection of a perimeter fence in return for the payment of the agreed sum of money. She is his client and he is providing her with a specified service.

The agreed day dawns and Jack arrives with two workers, Liam and Alan, and the three of them erect the fence. Liam and Alan are employees of Jack and he pays them a salary in return for their labour. Susan has no control over Liam and Alan, who follow Jack's instructions. If Susan wanted the fence to be erected in a certain way, she would need to talk to Jack, who would then tell Liam and Alan what to do. Susan has no right to give orders to Liam and Alan directly.

When the fence is complete and Susan is satisfied with the result, she will pay the agreed sum to Jack. Out of that money, Jack will pay a salary to Liam and to Alan, with the rest of the money going into his pocket.

There are two contracts in existence in this example. There is a contract for services between Susan and Jack, with Jack being an independent contractor, and there is a contract of service between Jack as employer and Liam and Alan as employees, who each have their own contract with Jack.

The importance of this distinction

It is important to determine whether a contract of service or a contract for services governs the relationship between parties for the following reasons:

- The contract of service has certain implied terms, for example the employer's extensive duties to ensure the safety of employees, and the employee's duty of fidelity towards the employer. This is not necessarily so in the contract for services.

- As a general rule, an employer owes a special duty of care to employees arising from the contract itself, but not to independent contractors.

- Most of the employment protection legislation applies only to employees. For example, the Unfair Dismissals Acts 1977 to 2007 and the Redundancy Payments Acts 1967 to 2007 apply only to employees.

- Employers in certain industries are required to pay a levy to FÁS in terms of the Industrial Training Act 1967. The value of the levy is calculated according to the number of employees at the employer's firm, but does not include the number of independent contractors.

- An employer is vicariously liable for the wrongs of an employee, but it is very seldom that an employer is liable for the wrongs of an independent contractor. The concept of vicarious liability will be examined in Chapter 15.

- As a general rule, trade unions represent employees rather than independent contractors.

- When a company goes into liquidation the employees of that company are protected as their outstanding wages are treated as preferred debts of the company. In other words, the employees will be placed near the beginning of the queue when it comes to the company paying the people to whom it owes money.

- Employees have their tax deducted from their salary by their employer, who must then pay that tax to the State. Independent contractors are responsible for paying their own tax.
- Perhaps the most important consequence of the type of contract is the question of dismissal, as an independent contractor cannot be dismissed. The Unfair Dismissals Acts only apply to employees. If a person is dismissed and goes to the Employment Appeals Tribunal claiming unfair dismissal, an employer might raise the defence that the person was not an employee and therefore cannot be dismissed.

In the development of employment law, the courts have, over time, applied a number of tests to determine whether a person was an employee or self-employed. The control test is probably the most established and best known. The court will examine the degree of control exercised by the purported employer and whether the purported employee agreed to that control or recognised the employer's right of control (in instances where the employee might have skills that are superior or distinct from those of the employer).

In the ever-changing marketplace, however, the control test proved inadequate to cater for all types of employment relationships and the courts went on to develop a variety of tests. For the purposes of this book it is not necessary to go into the history of those tests as the modern approach of the courts is to adopt a broad or 'big picture' approach and look for clues and indicators as to whether the contract under scrutiny is one of service or one for services.

In coming to a decision regarding the status of a person who claims to be an employee, the courts will ask questions such as:

- Who actually provides the services? If the engaged person is permitted to get somebody else to do all or any of the work contracted for, it is likely that the person is self-employed or an independent contractor. Generally, a contract of employment contemplates that an employee will provide his or her own work and skills and not those of somebody else.
- Does somebody have the power to engage and dismiss? If the alleged employer does not have the power or authority to 'hire or fire', then this is a good indication that the alleged employer is not, in law, the employer. This scenario would apply where there is a subcontractor hiring out labourers to a construction firm. However, if the construction firm exercises such close control over the work being done and pays the workers their wages and is entitled to dismiss those workers, then the court might hold that the workers have become the employees of the construction firm.
- Remuneration – who pays what to whom? An employee cannot contract to work for nothing. A contract of employment must contain an agreement that

one party will work for the other in consideration of a wage or other remuneration. Very often an employee will be paid according to the time spent at work (of service), whereas an independent contractor will be paid for a specific task (for services). Again, this test is not absolute as certain employees do get paid for specific tasks, for example piece workers.

- Working hours – can a person be forced to work at a certain time? As a general rule, an employee does not determine his or her own hours of work, but again, this test is not infallible, particularly with the introduction of flexi-time and working from home.

- Workplace – who supplies the premises? An employee generally works at premises supplied by the employer. Again, this test is not conclusive, for example the computer operator who works from home or, conversely, the subcontractor who works on the client's site.

- Tools of the trade – who supplies them? If the worker pays for his or her own tools, then this is often a strong indication that he or she is self-employed or an independent contractor. There are clear exceptions to this rule with many artisans preferring to buy their own tools, despite being employees. A tool allowance is a fairly common payment nowadays.

As there are so many variables, and these keep growing and evolving to adapt to the ever-changing workplace, the courts will look for clues and decide what the dominant impression is when scrutinising the relationship between the parties.

In the Supreme Court decision of *Henry Denny & Sons (Ireland) Ltd (t/a Kerry Foods) v Minister for Social Welfare* [1998] ELR 36, the court endorsed the approach that looks at the totality of factors in deciding the nature of the contract between the parties. Even where the written contract between the parties gives labels to that relationship, the court will not follow those labels where the facts indicate that the contract is different to what it is titled. This is necessary as parties could attempt to mislead third parties by describing their contract as one thing whilst knowing that actually it is another thing.

Commencing Employment

Anyone who works for an employer for a regular wage or salary automatically has a contract of employment, whether it is in written form or not. Section 23 of the Industrial Relations Act 1990 states that a contract of employment may be expressed or implied, oral or in writing.

Many of the terms of a contract of employment may emerge from the common law, statutes or collective agreements made through trade unions or may be derived from the custom or practice in a particular industry. It is therefore very important when you start a job to get in touch with your union representative to find out what collective agreements apply to you (as these usually set out conditions that are better than those provided by statute). It is your job to find these things out and the employer is entitled to assume that you know these things.

The Terms of Employment (Information) Acts 1994 and 2001 provide that an employer must furnish an employee with a written statement of certain particulars of the terms of employment. The Protection of Employees (Fixed-Term Work) Act 2003 provides that where an employer proposes to renew a fixed-term contract, the fixed-term employee shall be informed in writing by the employer of the objective grounds justifying the renewal of the fixed-term contract and the failure to offer a contract of indefinite duration, at the latest by the date of the renewal. Employers are required by the Unfair Dismissals Acts to give notice in writing to each employee, setting out the procedure that the employer will observe before, and for the purpose of, dismissing the employee. This must be given not later than twenty-eight days after entering into a contract of employment. The Payment of Wages Act 1991 gives every employee the right to a written statement every pay day with every deduction itemised.

The important principle to understand about any of these statutes that provide for certain details to be in writing is that they do not say that an employment contract is only a contract when it is in writing. That is not the law. The employment contract comes into existence when the parties agree on the terms of that contract, whether that is in writing, in words or simply by their behaviour.

The Terms of Employment (Information) Act provides that certain aspects and details of that established contract must be recorded in writing so that they are available not only to the parties themselves but to third parties, for example labour inspectors. It is also quite clear that the provisions of this Act apply to virtually any contract of employment, including employees working under a contract of apprenticeship, employed through an employment agency or employed by the State (this includes people employed by the HSE). The Act does not apply to employees who have only been employed (continuously) for less than one month (although, strangely, the Act says that the employer must provide this written statement of particulars to the employee within two months of the employee starting work). Before December 2001 the Act did not apply to employees who worked for less than eight hours per week, but this exclusion was removed by the Protection of Employees (Part-Time Work) Act 2001.

Other Important Statutes that Protect Employees

There are a number of other statutes that protect employees. It is beyond the scope of this book to go into any of these in detail, but it is important that nurses know about their existence.

The Minimum Notice and Terms of Employment Act 1973 provides that employees in continuous service with the same employer for at least thirteen weeks are entitled to a minimum period of notice before the employer may dismiss them. Prior to 20 December 2001 the Act did not apply to a person who was normally required to work for the employer for less than eight hours a week. However, from that date the Protection of Employees (Part-Time Work) Act 2001 removed the exclusion relating to the number of hours worked.

The Payment of Wages Act 1991 deals with issues such as modes of payment of wages, salary advices (wage slip) and deductions. This Act applies to all employees, including 'a person holding office, or in the service of, the State . . . or otherwise as a civil servant', and it therefore covers nurses working for the HSE or any other State body, and of course any nurse working in the private sector.

The Organisation of Working Time Act 1997 regulates hours of work, rest and lunch breaks, and holidays. The Act sets the minimum entitlement and parties are free to agree to longer breaks or more holidays. There are also collective agreements in a large number of industries setting out employees' entitlements to rest and meal breaks, overtime and annual holidays. This most certainly applies to the nursing sector. These collective agreements will, for example, vary the times at which rest is taken or vary the averaging period over which weekly working time is calculated. Again, it is very important when you start a job to find out exactly which collective agreements apply to you and what benefits they give you, or whether you are excluded from the provisions of this Act. In the absence of any agreements or specific clauses in your contract of employment, this Act sets out the minimum that you are entitled to – an employer is not allowed to offer you or give you less, unless that has been negotiated between your union and the employer, and sanctioned by the Minister for Enterprise, Trade and Innovation.

The National Minimum Wage Act 2000 sets out the rate of the minimum wage (which is changed from time to time). The Act applies to all employees, including full-time, part-time, temporary and casual employees, with the exception of apprentices and employees who are close relatives of the employer.

The Redundancy Payments Acts 1967 to 2007 oblige employers to pay compensation to employees dismissed for reasons of redundancy.

The Protection of Employees (Part-Time Work) Act 2001 applies to all part-time employees and ensures that they do not receive less than that obtained by their full-time counterparts or 'comparable employees' (in other words, other employees doing the same or similar work as the part-time employee). It also seeks to prevent abuse of the practice of 'rolling-over' of part-time contracts; a practice much favoured by government departments.

The Protection of Employees (Fixed-Term Work) Act 2003 is very similar in structure and content to the Protection of Employees (Part-Time Work) Act 2001. The 2003 Act applies to all fixed-term employees and ensures that they are not worse off than their colleagues on open-ended contracts ('permanent' employees).

Contract of employment: summary

1   The law distinguishes between two types of contract when looking at employment: the contract of service between an employer and an employee and the contract for services between an independent contractor and a client.

2   This distinction is important for a number of reasons. Most importantly, an independent contractor cannot be dismissed and a number of protective statutes only apply to employees.

3   The courts have formulated a number of tests to determine whether a contract is one for services or of service, but the modern approach is to look at the entire relationship and dealings between the parties and thereby gain a dominant impression of the nature of the relationship.

4   A contract of service between an employer and an employee can be agreed with a handshake, or in words, or in writing. The existence and validity of this contract does not depend on it being reduced to writing.

5   There are statutes directing the parties to a contract of service to record certain details of that contract in writing. These details do not create the contract, which is already in existence. The details are rather a written record of an existing contract so that the parties and others can refer to those written details when they are needed.

Further reading

Meenan, F. 'Protection of Employees (Fixed-Term Work) Act 2003 – recent case law', *Irish Employment Law Journal* 3 (2006), 39.

Useful websites

Department of Enterprise, Trade and Innovation: www.deti.ie
National Employment Rights Authority: www.employmentrights.ie
Irish Nurses and Midwives Organisation: www.inmo.ie
Impact (trade union): www.impact.ie/iopen24
Psychiatric Nurses Association of Ireland: www.pna.ie
Respiratory Nurses Association of Ireland: www.ncnm.ie/anail/index.asp
Irish Practice Nurses Association: www.irishpracticenurses.ie
International Council of Nurses: www.icn.ch

chapter 15

VICARIOUS LIABILITY AND THE NURSE

> *Learning outcomes*
> At the completion of this chapter the reader should know and understand:
> * The concept of vicarious liability in Irish law.
> * The concept of indemnity insurance and the impact of the Clinical Indemnity Scheme.

The Concept of Vicarious Liability

Vicarious liability simply means that one person is held liable for the wrongdoing of another. This concept is not limited to employment law. For example, a driver may be vicariously liable for the actions of a passenger, or a host for the actions of a guest, and in rare circumstances a parent for the actions of a child. Before a defendant can be found liable for the wrongs of another, the person for whom the defendant is vicariously liable must have acted negligently and the defendant must be in a position of control over that negligent person.

In this chapter, the specific question of employer liability for the torts of an employee will be examined. This is known as the doctrine of *respondeat superior*.

An employer will only be held liable for the negligent acts of an employee if that employee was acting in the course of his or her employment when carrying out the negligent act. The courts have not always been as precise as one would like when defining what is meant by the phrase 'in the course of employment', but essentially it means that if an employee is doing what he or she has been employed to do, irrespective of whether the employee is doing it well or not, the employer will be held liable for the negligent act, rather than the employee being held personally liable for the consequences of his or her actions. By the same token, where an employee is doing something that he or she has not been employed to do, the employer will escape liability.

In order to hold an employer liable for the actions of an employee, the plaintiff needs to prove three things:

* The wrongdoer is an employee of the employer being sued.
* The employee was negligent.
* The negligent action causing the damage was within the employee's scope (or course) of employment.

The first two aspects have been covered elsewhere in this book. The third requirement needs to be examined further. The scope or course of employment tests have been used interchangeably by the Irish courts when determining whether an employer should be held liable for the actions of an employee. This is unfortunate as there often seem to be conflicting interpretations of the two tests. The course of employment test is the more liberal of the two tests and takes into account the practicalities of the modern workplace. However, the scope of employment test is currently the dominant test in Irish law (although there may be changes coming as a result of the influence of English law), and this is a stricter test.

Put simply, the scope of employment test says that an employee is acting within the scope of his or her employment when an employer has authorised (expressly or impliedly) his or her actions. The narrowness of the test comes about through the principle that it is not enough for the plaintiff to show that the employee was acting within the authority of the employer, it must also be shown that those acts must be done for the employer.

The course of employment test says that an employee is acting within the course of employment when the employee is not only doing the job he or she was employed to do, but also where there is 'sufficient connection' between the wrongdoing and the employee's job. If such a connection is found, the employer is liable for the employee's wrongdoing. The employer is held liable not only for the acts of the employee, but also for the manner in which those acts were carried out. This has been the approach favoured by the English courts, which have found an employer liable for the following actions by an employee: a petrol tanker driver who threw away his cigarette whilst transferring petrol from the tanker to a tank; a bus driver who caused a collision whilst speeding; and employees who raced horses to the forge and injured a passer-by.

In *O'Keeffe v Hickey* [2008] IESC 72, the Supreme Court of Ireland held that an employer is vicariously liable for the acts of the employee only where a wrongful act was authorised by the employer or there was a wrongful and unauthorised mode of doing some authorised act.

Facts: O'Keeffe was a pupil at a national school and Hickey was the principal of the school and provided music lessons to O'Keeffe. During these lessons Hickey sexually abused O'Keeffe. O'Keeffe claimed that the Department of Education, as Hickey's employer, was vicariously liable for the actions of Hickey.

Issue before the court: Was Hickey acting within the scope of his employment?

Decision of the court: The majority of the Supreme Court decided that the Department of Education was not vicariously liable. However, this was based on their finding that Hickey was not considered an employee of the Department of Education because his contract was with the manager of the school.

The court was divided on the question of whether, if he had been an employee, Hickey's actions fell outside his scope of employment. Hardiman J adopted a very strict test and found that such acts could never be so closely connected to the teacher's employment as to be a mode of doing his job. On the other hand, Geoghegan J and Fennelly J found that under certain circumstances acts of sexual abuse by a school teacher could be considered to be acts that are committed during the course of employment.

O'Keeffe is the leading Irish case on vicarious liability but it illustrates the difficulty in interpreting the phrase 'within the scope (and course) of employment'. The court seemed to be using both tests, with some judges arriving at one decision and others disagreeing and finding differently. Unfortunately, the decision rested ultimately on the finding that the teacher was not an employee of the Department of Education.

Interestingly, in the English decision of *Lister v Lesley Hall* [2002] 1 AC 215, on facts very similar to *O'Keeffe*, and on reasoning very similar to that adopted by Geoghegan J and Fennelly J, the House of Lords found that there was sufficient connection between the employment (boarding school warden) and the wrong (sexual abuse) to find the employer vicariously liable.

If deciding whether a health authority or a hospital is liable for the actions of a nurse, then the same questions would need to be asked. Was the nurse carrying out a wrongful act (impliedly) authorised by the employer (the scope test) or was it a wrongful and unauthorised mode of doing some authorised act (the course test)?

Clinical Indemnity Scheme (CIS)

Indemnity insurance is a scheme whereby the insurer agrees to indemnify the insured against the loss that would be caused by the type of risk that is insured against. In the case of indemnity insurance for the vicarious liability of an employer for the actions of a nurse, the risk is clinical negligence.

The State-funded Clinical Indemnity Scheme (CIS) provides an indemnity to health agencies, funded in whole or in part by the taxpayer, against the cost of claims brought against them for personal injury arising from clinical negligence. It has been established on the principle of enterprise liability, which means that a public hospital covered by the CIS assumes vicarious liability for the acts and omissions of its employees (specifically its clinical staff and, since 2004, its consultant doctors) providing clinical services.

The distinguishing feature of enterprise liability is that the plaintiff does not sue the individual health professional as the agency agrees to take vicarious responsibility for its clinical staff. In other words, vicarious liability is admitted by the employer and does not have to be proven by the plaintiff-patient, provided, of course, that the actions of the employee are regarded as the provision of clinical services and therefore covered by the CIS policy. It does not matter, in practical terms, whether the employer is vicariously liable or whether the employee is directly liable because, once it confirms that the action falls under the auspices of the CIS, the State Claims Agency takes over the administration of the defence.

The stated benefit of this arrangement is that it will not be necessary to have a number of co-defendants in a medical malpractice action – for example, Minister for Health, health board and health professional – as only one defendant, the CIS, will be sued. This will save on the trauma and expense of separate defendants with separate legal representation and will hopefully mean fewer and/or shorter trials. This is good news for those employees whose actions are clearly covered by the scheme. However, the confusing series of tests to decide vicarious liability in the common law has been replaced by a new confusion in deciding whether the employee's actions are covered by the scheme.

The CIS covers all claims alleging medical malpractice or clinical negligence against an agency and/or its staff arising from the delivery of professional medical services. It will therefore cover services provided at hospitals, clinics and other facilities owned or operated by the Health Service Executive (HSE) as well as services delivered in patients' homes and other community facilities, under the auspices of the HSE or other similar agencies.

In terms of the National Treasury Management Agency (Delegation of Functions) Order 2003, 'professional medical services' means:

(a) services provided by registered medical practitioners or registered dentists of a diagnostic or palliative nature, or consisting of the provision of treatment in respect of any illness, disease, injury or other medical condition,

(b) services provided by other health professionals in the performance of their duties, including pharmacists, nurses, midwives, paramedics, ambulance personnel, laboratory technicians, or

(c) services connected with the provision of health or medical care provided by persons acting under the direction of a person to whom paragraph (a) or (b) applies.

Another problem with the CIS cover that has caused a lot of controversy concerns so-called 'Good Samaritan' acts such as stopping to help an injured motorist. The CIS only covers claims arising from Good Samaritan acts that occur in an agency's premises. It does not cover Good Samaritan acts that take place elsewhere.

In addition, the CIS does not cover the costs of representation before a disciplinary body such as a fitness to practise inquiry.

In instances where the CIS does not cover the employee's actions, it is not clear whether the common law of vicarious liability still operates in medical or clinical negligence cases or whether the employee will be personally liable for these actions. The better approach would seem to be that the common law cannot be excluded where the statutory scheme does not go as far as the common law.

If the common law action based on vicarious liability is excluded, it will mean that employees, including nurses, need to have indemnity insurance to cover those situations that are not covered by the CIS policy. It also means that if a nurse wanted to ensure proper legal representation at a disciplinary hearing or a criminal court hearing, he or she would need either to pay the fees involved or to have an insurance policy to cover such a situation.

Vicarious liability: summary

1 The principle of vicarious liability is that one person is held liable for the actions of another.

2 As a general rule, an employer will be held liable for the actions of an employee 'in the course and scope of employment'.

3 In deciding what actions are in the course of employment, the Irish courts have a two-legged test that includes both the 'course test' and the 'scope test'. Is the act a wrongful act (expressly or impliedly) authorised by the employer or is the act a wrongful and unauthorised mode of doing some authorised act?

4 The two tests can yield different results and there is uncertainty in Irish law as to which is the dominant test.

5 The Clinical Indemnity Scheme (CIS), which is based on enterprise liability, rests on the premise that the employer will admit vicarious liability if the negligent actions of the employee fall within the bounds of 'professional medical services' as defined.

6 The CIS does not cover the cost of legal fees for disciplinary proceedings or for criminal trials.

Further reading

Commission on Patient Safety and Quality Assurance *Building a Culture of Patient Safety* [Madden Report], Dublin: Department of Health and Children, 2008.

McElhinney, J. and Healy, S. 'Clinical risk management in Ireland', *Medico-Legal Journal of Ireland* 9 (2003), 70–75.

Oglesby, A. M. 'An overview of the clinical indemnity scheme and clinical risk management in Ireland', *Clinical Risk* 16 (2010), 127–9.

Sheikh, A. A. and Cusack, D. A. 'Clinical risk management in Ireland: the status quo, reform and a need to grapple with the basics', *Medico-Legal Journal of Ireland* 9 (2003), 62–9.

Useful websites

Clinical Indemnity Scheme: www.stateclaims.ie/ClinicalIndemnityScheme/introduction.html

Royal College of Physicians of Ireland: www.rcpi.ie

Medical Protection Society: www.medicalprotection.org

Malcomson Law (solicitors): www.mlaw.ie

chapter 16

TERMINATION OF THE EMPLOYMENT CONTRACT

> ### Learning outcomes
> At the completion of this chapter the reader should know and understand:
> - The difference between termination of an employment contract by dismissal and termination by the expiry of an employment contract.
> - The types of dismissal recognised by the common law.
> - The provisions of the Unfair Dismissals Acts 1977 to 2007 and their application to nurses in Ireland.

Termination by Expiration and Termination by Dismissal

An employment contract expires or ceases to exist because either the parties to that contract agree it should end or the contract itself specifies that it shall end on a stipulated date or at the completion of a stipulated task. An employment contract will also expire if one of the parties dies, because in a personal contract the specified identity of the parties to that contract is an essential part of the contract.

A dismissal will occur when one party unilaterally ends the emloyment contract, without agreement by the other party. The party that unilaterally ends an employment contract in a dismissal is usually the employer. An exception is the case of constructive dismissal, where the employee ends the contract but the circumstances surrounding the resignation are such that the law deems it a dismissal.

Disputes between employees and employers concerning dismissal are usually about whether a dismissal has actually taken place or, if the dismissal is admitted or proved, whether that dismissal was fair and lawful.

Before looking at the question of dismissal, it might be helpful to consider briefly the internal procedures that are usually followed before a dismissal takes place. As most nurses are employed in the public sector, the focus will be on developments within that sphere. However, many private nursing homes and hospitals will use similar procedures.

There have been substantial developments regarding the disciplinary procedures applied to civil servants, who are now protected by the Unfair Dismissals Acts 1977 to 2007 and Circular 14 of 2006, which contained a new disciplinary code. However, nurses are not defined as civil servants, despite being in the employment of a public agency.

Nurses are accordingly still subject to the cumbersome disciplinary and dismissal procedure originally set out in the Health Act 1970, as opposed to the more streamlined procedure now available to civil servants. However, nurses who are both temporary and permanent officers of the Health Service Executive (HSE) are at least protected by the Unfair Dismissals Acts, with a route of appeal to the Employment Appeals Tribunal (EAT) and ultimately the courts. This is the situation since 'officers of the health board' were removed from the exclusion section of the Unfair Dismissals Acts.

The HSE has made matters a lot easier for its employees by producing an 'Employees' Handbook', which details the disciplinary and grievance procedures applicable to employees of the HSE. The handbook does not distinguish between officers and employees and it must be assumed that 'employee' is a generic term covering all those in the employ of the HSE. For the purposes of dismissal law, the distinction is in any event academic, but it might be worth clarification in other areas of employment law such as redundancy and transfers.

The handbook has the following to say about the disciplinary procedure:

> The Disciplinary Procedure is a staged procedure. The following principles underpin the procedure:
> - Every effort will be made by the Employee's immediate Manager to address shortcomings in work standards, conduct or attendance through informal counselling without invoking the Disciplinary Procedure;
> - While the Disciplinary Procedure will normally be operated on a progressive basis, in cases of serious misconduct the Manager may bypass Stages 1, 2 and 3 of the Procedure;
> - No decision regarding disciplinary action will be made until a formal disciplinary hearing has been convened and the Employee has been afforded an opportunity to respond;
> - The Employee will be advised of his or her right to be accompanied by a work colleague or trade union representative at any meeting under the formal Disciplinary Procedure;
> - The Employee will be advised in advance of the disciplinary hearing of the precise nature of the complaint against him or her and will be given copies of any relevant documentation;
> - The Employee will be afforded the opportunity to state his or her case and challenge any evidence that may be relied upon in reaching a decision;
> - An Employee may appeal the outcome of the disciplinary hearing.

Stages 1, 2 and 3 of the procedure refer respectively to an oral warning, a written warning and a final written warning. In cases of serious misconduct, there is a chance of summary dismissal, which involves going directly to Stage 4: dismissal or action short of dismissal. Where a disciplinary hearing is held in terms of Stage 4 (i.e. where dismissal is a possibility), the decision maker will be the relevant national director. The handbook says that the 'National Director, PCCC may delegate authority to an Assistant National Director PCCC and the National Director NHO may delegate authority to an Assistant National Director NHO'. The outcome of the disciplinary hearing may be dismissal or action short of dismissal (for example, suspension without pay or demotion).

Types of Dismissal

The common law of dismissal has for all intents and purposes been overtaken by statutory law. Of course the interpretations by the courts of these statutory provisions form part of the common law. The different classifications of dismissal are still used and these were originally formulated by the courts and are part of the common law.

The types of dismissal recognised by the modern law are wrongful dismissal, unfair dismissal, lawful dismissal, summary dismissal and constructive dismissal.

Wrongful dismissal

An employee will allege wrongful dismissal when the termination has breached (broken) a term of the contract. For example, if a contract provides that an employee must be given three months' notice and the employer terminates the contract after one month's notice, then the employee can claim wrongful dismissal. This is an alternative cause of action to unfair dismissal and is the most popular cause of action after an action for unfair dismissal because it is based on the terms of the employment contract. This means that the usual contractual remedies apply, namely specific performance or damages.

The remedy of specific performance orders the wrongful party, in this case the employer, to fulfil its duties arising from the contract, which means that the employer must allow the employee to continue working as before. If a nurse has a dispute with an immediate superior and is wrongfully dismissed as a result, specific performance is possible if the nurse (or the superior) was transferred to another hospital or even to another wing of the same hospital, thereby avoiding contact and further conflict.

The other available remedy is damages. The Unfair Dismissals Acts place a limit or ceiling on the amount of damages an employee is entitled to receive when unfairly dismissed. However, if one brings an action based on wrongful dismissal in the Circuit Court, the amount of damages that may be awarded could substantially exceed the limit of two years' salary imposed by the Acts.

Lawful dismissal

A lawful dismissal is one that complies with the express and implied provisions of the contract between the parties, including terms imported into the contract by statute. For example, a dismissal with proper notice would be a lawful dismissal. However, the definition of unfair dismissal means that although a dismissal is lawful, it may still be unfair if, for example, it was for an arbitrary reason or due to an ulterior motive.

Summary dismissal

Summary dismissal occurs when the employer brings the contract to an immediate end without first giving lesser punishments such as a written warning. This usually happens in cases of serious misconduct such as the assault of a fellow employee or theft from the employer. The employee's actions must be such that the employer cannot be expected to continue the contract.

Constructive dismissal

This type of dismissal differs from the others as the employee, and not the employer, brings the contract to an end. In other words, the employee resigns. Under normal circumstances, a resignation is the employee's way of unilaterally ending an employment contract and would be the opposite of a dismissal. However, a constructive dismissal occurs if the employee resigns because the employer acted in such a way that it was intolerable for the employee to continue working. The employer's conduct is effectively the cause of the termination.

The test for this type of dismissal is an objective one. For example, an overly sensitive employee could not claim constructive dismissal after resigning as a result of the employer raising his voice at the employee. The employer's conduct that forced the employee to resign must be objectively improper or unlawful and must be in a manner calculated to destroy or seriously damage the relationship of confidence and trust with the employee. Examples would be a dramatic cut in pay without warning or explanation, a significant change in a job description (usually to a worse job) or a relocation to some remote branch of the employer's organisation that forces the employee to travel a considerable distance to get to and from work.

As it is an objective test, the court will look at the surrounding circumstances. In times of high unemployment, employees may be expected to 'grin and bear' a lot more on the grounds that they at least have a job.

Unfair dismissal

Even in cases where the employer sticks to the letter of the contract by giving proper notice and making any payments that are due, the employee can still allege unfair dismissal if the reason for that contract being terminated is an arbitrary or unfair reason. For example, if the employer did not like the employee's dress sense or religious beliefs – something that is not connected with the employee's ability to perform the job.

This type of dismissal was not recognised by the common law, where an employer could dismiss an employee for virtually any reason as long as the terms of the contract relating to notice or severance pay were fulfilled. As this situation left most employees extremely vulnerable to the whim of their employer, the question of unfair dismissals was extensively regulated by the Unfair Dismissals Acts.

Unfair Dismissals Acts 1977 to 2007

The Unfair Dismissals Acts protect employees from being unfairly dismissed and set out the rules by which dismissals are judged. Where an employee is unfairly dismissed, the Acts have created an adjudication system to allow the employee to seek justice and redress. The principal Act is the 1977 Act, with the 1993, 2001 and 2007 Acts making some important amendments.

Section 1 of the 1977 Act contains an extended definition of dismissal, which goes further than the common law. Paragraph (a) of the definition covers the situation where the employer unilaterally ends the contract, either with notice or summarily. This is obviously the most common form of dismissal. Paragraph (b) describes constructive dismissal. Paragraph (c) describes the dismissal of an employee on a fixed-term or specific-purpose contract. It is important to note that the expiration of such a contract is not the moment of dismissal, which happens when the employer fails to replace the expired contract with another fixed-term or specific-purpose contract of the same or similar nature.

This definition only tells us what a dismissal is. It does not define whether that dismissal is fair or lawful. The fairness or otherwise can only be determined once the existence of the dismissal is established.

Excluded employees

Section 2 of the 1977 Act excludes certain employees from the protection of the Act. These include an employee who has not worked continuously for the same employer for one year; an employee reaching the normal retirement age; a person employed by a family member or relative to work in a domestic setting or farm where both employer and employee reside; a person in employment as a member of the Defence Forces; the Judge Advocate-General; the chairperson of the Army Pensions Board or an ordinary member thereof who is not an officer of the Medical Corps of the Defence Forces; a member of An Garda Síochána; an apprentice or trainee on a training allowance; a manager of a local authority; officers of a vocational education committee; civil servants appointed directly by the government (as opposed to working for a government department); and the chief executive officer of the HSE.

The various categories that are excluded are self-explanatory with the exception perhaps of paragraph 1(a) of Section 2, which says that employees with less than one year's service are not protected by the Act unless the dismissal is in contravention of another statute. It would seem to be open to an employer to avoid the Act by making sure that an employee never has more than one year's service. For example, an employer might employ the same person for a considerable length of time, but always on six-month contracts with perhaps a couple of weeks' break between each contract. If the employee is dismissed and claims unfair dismissal, then the employer can argue that the person was employed for only six months and therefore is not protected by the Act.

The Unfair Dismissals (Amendment) Act 1993 addressed this exclusion section by saying that a Rights Commissioner, the Employment Appeals Tribunal or the Circuit Court may decide whether the employment of a person on a series of two or more contracts of employment between which there was a break of no more than twenty-six weeks was for the purpose of avoiding the provisions of the Unfair

Dismissals Acts. If it is decided that the motive behind this series of fixed-term or specific-purpose contracts was to avoid liability under the Act, the length of these various contracts may be added together to calculate the length of service of the employee and so to decide whether that employee is protected by the Act.

Persons engaged through employment agencies are covered by the Unfair Dismissals Acts. For the purposes of the Act, the person for whom the hired employee works is deemed to be the employer of that employee. This means that an agency nurse is protected by the Act: the nurse is employed by an employment agency to work in a hospital and therefore the hospital is deemed to be the employer of the nurse.

The Act does not apply to the dismissal of an employee who is standing in for another employee on statutory leave, provided that the employer informed the replacement employee, in writing, at the beginning of the job that his or her employment would terminate when the employee on leave returns.

Also, Section 3 reminds us that the Act does not apply to the dismissal of employees in their probation and training period, which is of one year or less. Section 3(2) states that the Act shall not apply to the dismissal of a nurse during the period when the nurse starts the job and is undergoing training for the purpose of becoming qualified or registered.

People employed by health boards as officers were previously specifically excluded by the Act, along with civil servants, but this is no longer the case, although their appointment, remuneration and discipline are still governed by the Health Act 1970.

Proving the fairness of the dismissal

Section 6 of the 1977 Act says that every dismissal of an employee will be deemed (presumed) to have been unfair unless the employer can show substantial grounds justifying the dismissal. In order to justify a dismissal, an employer must show that it resulted from one or more of the causes listed in Section 6(4) of the Act. These are:

- The capability, competence or qualifications of the employee. These are 'incapacity dismissals' and arise when an employee is unable to do the job he or she was originally employed to do.
- The employee's conduct (or usually misconduct). The employer must show that the employee's conduct was such that it warranted dismissal (substantive fairness) and that the procedures used to establish the grounds for that employee's dismissal were fair (procedural fairness).
- The redundancy of the employee occurs as a result of the employer ceasing to trade or carry on business, or where the employee's function is no longer required by the business of the employer, or where the employer must reduce the workforce, or where the work that the employee used to do must now be performed by somebody with superior qualifications.
- The fact that continuation of the employment would contravene another

statutory requirement. In other words, the existence of the employment contract contravenes a law.

- There were other substantial grounds for dismissal. This final category, stated in Section 6(6), is a 'catch-all' category to cover those dismissals that do not fit in any of the other categories. An example would be where the employee's continued employment poses a threat to the employer's business.

An employer who has dismissed an employee must, if asked, furnish in writing within fourteen days the reason for the dismissal.

Types of unfair dismissal

Section 6(2) of the 1977 Act, as amended, states that dismissals are deemed unfair under the Acts where it is shown that they are the result of one or more of the following grounds:

(a) The employee's trade union membership or activities, either outside working hours or at those times during working hours when permitted by the employer.
(b) The religious or political opinions of the employee.
(c) The race or colour or sexual orientation of the employee.
(d) Legal proceedings against the employer where the employee is a party or a witness.
(e) The unfair selection of the employee for redundancy, where the reason for the selection was based on a prohibited ground.
(f) The employee's pregnancy, the employee having recently given birth, because the employee is breastfeeding or any matters connected with pregnancy, birth or breastfeeding.
(g) The exercise or proposed exercise by the employee of the right to leave in terms of the Maternity Protection Act 1994.
(h) The exercise or proposed exercise by the employee of the right to leave in terms of the Adoptive Leave Act 1995.
(i) The exercise or proposed exercise by the employee of the right to leave in terms of the Parental Leave Act 1998.
(j) The age of the employee.
(k) The employee's membership of the Travelling community.
(l) The employee's rights or proposed exercise of rights under the National Minimum Wage Act 2000.
(m) The exercise or proposed exercise by the employee of the right to leave in terms of the Carer's Leave Act 2001.

As Section 6 already states that dismissals are deemed unfair until the employer can show otherwise, why are these special categories only deemed unfair, and not illegal? In other countries, for example South Africa, such dismissals are called 'automatically unfair dismissals' and the employer is not allowed to argue that they could ever be justified.

Irish society generally frowns on discriminatory practices and an employer will have quite a job convincing a tribunal or court that its actions were justified. This seems to be the real difference between dismissals under this section and the 'ordinary' dismissals under Section 6(4). With dismissals under this section the employer will need to lead more compelling evidence to justify the dismissal.

Employees claiming dismissal due to (a), (f), (g), (h), (i), (l) or (m) above may bring an unfair dismissal claim even though they do not have one year's continuous service with that employer. This is the other important distinction between dismissals under Section 6(2) and dismissals under Section 6(4).

Remedies for unfair dismissal

Under Section 7(1) of the 1977 Act, an employee found to have been unfairly dismissed is entitled to one of three forms of redress:

- Re-instatement in the original position. In other words, the employee is returned to his or her original job as if the dismissal had never taken place.
- Re-engagement in a suitable alternative job on conditions that a tribunal considers reasonable (as close as possible to the original position, at least as concerns salary and benefits and length of service). This might be the case where the employee's original position no longer exists and the only relief available is a similar job with the same employer on similar terms.
- Financial compensation up to a maximum of two years' pay. The amount of compensation will depend on factors such as the reasons for the dismissal, whether the employee was in any way at fault, whether the employee tried to minimise his or her loss by looking for another job and whether there was procedural fairness leading up to the dismissal.

An employee found to have been unfairly dismissed but who has suffered no financial loss may be awarded up to four weeks' pay. This usually occurs where the employee immediately found another job. Despite not suffering any financial loss, the employee can still receive token compensation, more for the purpose of reprimanding the employer than significantly compensating the employee.

How to claim under the Acts

An employee who claims to be unfairly dismissed and wishes to challenge the dismissal under the Acts must lodge a written claim within six months of the dismissal with a Rights Commissioner. If either the employer or the employee objects to the matter being heard by a Rights Commissioner, an application can be made directly to the Employment Appeals Tribunal. In exceptional circumstances the time limit for lodging an application can be extended for up to one year.

Termination: summary

1   An employment contract can be terminated by one party, or it may expire when its purpose is concluded or if the parties agree that it shall end.

2   In terms of the common law, a party could unilaterally terminate an employment contract for any reason as long as the procedure of termination was in accordance with the provisions of the contract (usually notice periods and severance payments).

3   As this meant that employees were extremely vulnerable, the Unfair Dismissals Act was created to ensure that a dismissal must be both substantively and procedurally fair.

4   An employee alleging unfair dismissal can have his or her case heard by a specialised tribunal called the Employment Appeals Tribunal (EAT).

5   If a dismissal is found to be unfair, the employee can be reinstated into his or her previous position, or re-engaged in a similar position, or financially compensated.

6   The above provisions now apply to all nurses, in both the public and the private sectors.

Useful websites
Employment Appeals Tribunal: www.eatribunal.ie

INDEX